KINGDOM
of LOVING

Walking in the Divine Love of Christ

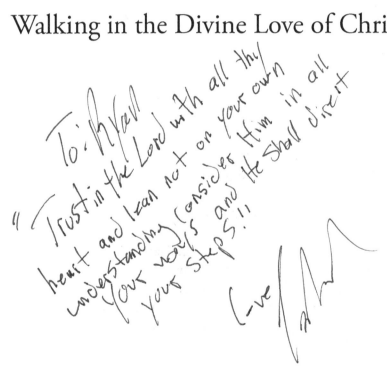

To: Ryan
" Trust in the Lord with all thy heart and lean not on your own understanding consider Him in all your ways and He shall direct your steps!!

Love [signature]

EMAN NORMAN

ISBN 978-1-0980-6689-5 (paperback)
ISBN 978-1-0980-6690-1 (digital)

Christian Faith Publishing, Inc.
832 Park Avenue
Meadville, PA 16335
www.christianfaithpublishing.com

Printed in the United States of America

ACKNOWLEDGMENTS

I would like to thank God most of all for asking me to write this book. He is truly my best friend.

I would also like to thank my daughter Laila for helping me with the title. You are one of the most beautiful and strongest girls I know. I love you forever.

Dearest thanks to Nicole, who encouraged me so much and also single handedly with the Lord got me out of a four-year writer's block with her tough love. She also did the first edit on this book in the midst of enduring many pains and hardships in her own life. I love you and am forever grateful for you.

Thank you to all the people along the way who encouraged me to finish or who provided a place for me to write without disruption. You know who you are, thank you.

INTRODUCTION

Jesus is truly amazing! He does amazing things. He comes wherever we are no matter what we are doing, and He dwells with us no matter what. He is willing and mighty to save us in His compassion for us. His love for us is without fail and unconditional. He rejoices over us with gladness by singing over us in joy. This is an incredible reality. Just think about God singing over us with His gladness, especially when we are going through trials and hardships. It's so comforting just to think about. In fact, before you go any further just try that. Think about God, the creator of the universe and everything in it, singing over you. *Selah*. Yes! King Jesus is singing over you and me, shedding light on the attitude He wants us to have.

So many have such a hard time receiving this kind of love that the reality of giving it seems impossible. I believe there is a simplicity to God's Word that is revealed in its fullness by the power of the Holy Spirit. This enables us to not only receive His unrelenting love for us but also give this unconditional love to everyone we encounter including ourselves.

We are in a kingdom, and it belongs to Jesus. It's the king's domain which is righteousness, joy, and peace in the Holy Ghost. We must stand in this reality. We must operate as sons and daughters in this kingdom as servants of His mighty love in righteousness with joy. There are many different ways to look into what this looks like in the life of a believer and how that is manifested on a daily basis. Like everything else, the foundation of this truth must be established in us to truly walk like Jesus walks.

And provide for those who grieve in Zion—to
bestow on them a crown of beauty instead of ashes,

the oil of joy instead of mourning, and a garment of praise instead of a spirit of despair. They will be called oaks of righteousness, A planting of the LORD for the display of His splendor. (Isaiah 61:3 NIV)

When He looks at us, the eyes of our Lord sees beauty—pure, unblemished, and radiant beauty! He sees what we look like with His Son, Jesus, living in us. He always sees us with divine purpose and destiny. Jesus is the finished work living in us for those who believe in Him. He is passionate about us seeing the same finished work in ourselves. We must realize that there are no more ashes, for God has bestowed on us a crown of beauty. Many people believe a lie that makes them see themselves as hopeless and broken, full of despair, and unloved. They feel abandoned and unwanted, unattractive and insecure in themselves. When one believes these lies, they are robbed and blinded from seeing the true beauty in which we are made. He created us in His own image and after His own likeness. And there is nothing ugly in Him. (See Genesis 1:27.)

The trials of life that we are promised will come, sometimes causing great mourning and tears. The pressures of this life can overwhelm us and overtake us. This occurs in finances, relationships, marriages, and even callings and promises on our lives from the Lord. We need to hear from Him about how to deal with the troubles in this world.

"I have said these things to you, that in me you may have peace. In the world you will have tribulation. But take heart; I have overcome the world" (John 16:33).

Notice that Jesus promises we will have tribulation in this world. However, His desire and will is that we would have peace because He has *overcome* the world. In other words, He has defeated the power and authority of the enemy that takes our peace. In defeating the enemy, Jesus has secured us in Him and assures us that He will give us His own peace and not as the world gives. (See John 14:27.) We can stand in the midst of great trials and be at perfect peace because Jesus is Lord over all.

Isaiah 61:3 says that He gives us the oil of gladness instead of mourning. Gladness of heart is one of the hardest things I have found to keep during trials. But I've realized after each trial I'm able to endure more and to keep my joy more and more as the testing of life come. We really have two options during trials. We can take our eyes and hearts off of Jesus and be tried in the fire and get burned or we can keep our eyes and hearts on the Lord. Trusting in His love for us and walking out of the fiery trial without even smelling like smoke. Let's wear the garment of praise instead of a faint, crippled spirit even if it feels like we are going to faint. The Holy Spirit is faithful and true to clothe us with a garment of praise so that we may be called "oaks of righteousness" by His Spirit.

"Wait on the LORD: Be of good courage, And He shall strengthen thine heart: Wait; I say, on the LORD" (Psalms 27:14).

We wait on the Lord by being still and knowing He is God. We must allow adoration to arise in our hearts towards Him. Let's do that right now. Be still in His presence. Let the Holy Spirit move your heart and affection towards Jesus for who He is. Selah.

He is our king and how mighty His love is for us. He will strengthen our hearts. We are the righteousness of God in Christ Jesus. This is not our idea. This is God's idea, and He is the one who has made it to be true. We must believe this truth no matter what we are going through or how much we think we've messed up God's plan for our lives. As we live in repentance, how can we mess it up? He's the author of your life, and He is worthy of praise, honor, glory, and thanksgiving no matter how we feel. He is worthy of our praise.

He is mighty to save and redeem us from all unrighteousness. This is not to say it's okay to disobey God and live in sin because that's never okay. It's living in spiritual paralysis that keeps the righteous man from getting back up because he doesn't see how valuable he is in God's eyes. Our Heavenly Father sees His Son's blood when He looks at us. We are pure in His sight. We must see the same thing God sees when we look at ourselves. We must believe we are worth the price He paid to purify our hearts in His truth. This transforms us into new creations, holy and acceptable to God. We are the planting of the Lord that He may be glorified.

"Love people with eternity in mind, because this world is passing away" (Peter 2:11; Hebrews 13:14–21).

There is only one thing in life that's permeating through the physical and spiritual, surpassing logic and redefining existence. As the cosmic thread, the love of God reigns supreme. It moves the hearts of men and creates in us the ability to see and believe the truth. There is only one Truth and He is alive and His motive is love. His heart is towards us at all times. He has great pleasure when He sees our faith in Him working through His matchless love.

"The Lord your God is in your midst, a mighty one who will save; He will rejoice over you with gladness; He will quiet you by His love; He will exult over you with loud singing" (Zephaniah 3:17 ESV).

CHAPTER 1

PICK UP YOUR CROSS

Strengthen us, Lord, to come boldly to your throne with peace and confidence that You have the power to do what You say You will do. Empower us with encouragement by Your Holy Spirit. Give us a faith in You, Jesus, that our hope will be firmly in Your name. Amen.

Every promise from God requires faith to obtain it. This has already been established in us by the power of the Holy Spirit. We activate this faith when we thank Him for His promises and rejoice in His faithfulness before we ever see the promise manifested. We should proclaim and declare in peace and confidence the promises made to us by our Father with thanksgiving. It's not that God needs reminding but rather that our faith needs to be exercised so that we can grow from faith to faith and from truth to truth.

In the depths of a man's soul and heart, there is a war of faith to believe the truth about who Jesus is and who He says we are. This is the true battle. The war is against unbelief. The enemy is relentless in his quest to destroy the faith of the children of God. Just think… he does not know when his time is up. This motivates him to take as many people with him as possible. He never rests. But the armor of God truly defeats the works of the enemy. We are oaks of righteousness so that we may stand in faith and bring glory to God. When we begin to sink into the depths and waves are crashing against us, it's hard to keep our eyes on Jesus. We must stand and keep standing.

We must contend for hope and come into agreement with the truth who has already set us free.

"True belief and faith in the reality of Jesus will keep you on your knees in a place of surrender."

> *Keep your life free from the love of money, and be content with what you have, for He has said, "I will never leave you nor forsake you." So that we can confidently say,*
> *"The Lord is my helper;*
> *I will not fear,*
> *What can man do to me?" (Hebrews 13:5–6)*

How can we fear and yet remain confident in Christ? Fear is rooted in uncertainty, which is rooted in self-preservation. Remember the first thing that Jesus tells us to do is to deny ourselves, first, pick up our cross, and follow Him.

> *And He said to all, "If anyone would come after Me, let him deny himself and take up his cross daily and follow me. For whoever would save his life will lose it, but whoever loses his life for my sake will save it. For what does it profit a man if he gains the whole world and loses or forfeits himself? For whoever is ashamed of me and of My words, of him will the Son of Man be ashamed when He comes in His Glory and the Glory of the Father and of the holy angels." (Matthew 16:24–26)*

Jesus says if we lose our life, we will find it. We get to become a living sacrifice to the Lord. We lose our life and gain His life. In this, we get to truly live. Jesus *is* life and the one who has Jesus *has* life, but the one who does *not* have Jesus does *not* have life.

"In him was life and the life was the light of man" (John 1:4).

"Selflessness is required for love to thrive in kingdom atmosphere."

In order to truly love God with all that we are and love others as we love ourselves, we must become selfless. The only way to become selfless is to believe that the life of Jesus is far greater than your own. He gave His life up to give it to us. This is good news! Jesus gave His life for us so that we could live out His life in place of our own. It's not good news if you have to earn it. People get caught up and run in circles trying to serve God to preserve their own lives.

"There is a way that seems right to a man but its end is they way to death" (Proverbs 14:12).

Religion tells us that one must try to maintain and earn what Jesus paid a price for us to walk in freely. We obtain this by receiving salvation by faith in Christ. The Galatians tried to do this when they began practicing religious exercises to try to maintain their salvation. They tried to elevate themselves instead of exalting God. I'm referring to salvation, which means *saved,* not righteousness (being right with God). There is a difference. How can we maintain a free gift? If you didn't do anything to earn it, what makes you think you must do something (or not do something) to maintain it? It's deception to think this way, and this leads us away from walking in the Spirit and being led by the Spirit who dwells in us and wants to lead us into all truth.

Jesus' Spirit lives in those who believe in Him—the name which is above every name, the anointed One, the Word made flesh, the King of kings and Lord of lords, the Prince of peace, the Everlasting Father, the only begotten Son of God. He was love walking among us, and now He is love living *in* us and walking *with* us. Jesus gave up His life here on this earth. By doing so, He has richly blessed us with His love and brought us into the kingdom of heaven through His blood and our faith in Him. He has given us the ultimate gift in the Holy Spirit. He is *our* seal, *our* comforter, *our* teacher, and *our* guide. He is mighty. He is power, He is God. He is amazing!

All confidence in Christ comes through the Holy Spirit. Think of the disciples leaving Jesus and Peter denying Him three times. After the Holy Spirit and power came into the upper room, things changed. (See Acts 2.) In Matthew 3:11, we hear John the Baptist proclaim how Jesus will baptize us with the Holy Spirit and fire. I believe being baptized in the Holy Spirit is being transformed by him into a new creation.

> *I came to cast fire on the earth, and would*
> *that it were already kindled! I have a baptism to be*
> *baptized with, and how great is my distress until it*
> *is accomplished! (Luke 12:49–50)*

I remember when I was filled with the Holy Spirit and fire. I had a vision in the night in 2008. In the vision, I was in a church, and there was a man preaching there whom I had never seen before. He was wearing an all-white suit. He was very passionate. He had bright blue eyes that cut through everything they touched. Then all of a sudden, he stopped and looked right at me, pointing his finger at me. He made his way down the platform coming straight at me with his finger still straight at my head. As he got closer, I could feel the presence and power and fear of the Lord all around me. He walked right up to me, speaking in tongues, and touched me on my forehead with his finger that had been pointing at me. It was like a lightning bolt, full of lightning bolts, shot through my body, and from my innermost being, I burst and began speaking in tongues. As I was speaking in tongues in the vision, I awoke from my sleep still speaking in tongues and sat straight up in my bed!

This transformation that takes place in a believer is one of complete and total newness of life. It changes even the appearance of a person because the Spirit is greater than the outward reflection. After you become baptized in the Holy Spirit, your reflection that you have dies with Christ, and you come alive with Him in true life. There is a reason people say that after being saved, their appearance and countenance changes. This transformation empowers us to never look back or see ourselves as anything less than a redeemed child of God, spotless and blameless before Him. This is our confidence in Christ—that Christ dwells in us and hope comes alive!

If you have never been baptized in the Holy Spirit and fire, being transformed into God's new creation, and you want to, pray with me. Ask Jesus this right now. Just simply say, "Jesus, I believe in you. Baptize me in your Holy Spirit and fire. Holy Spirit, come and fill me right now in resurrection power and the fire of God's love in Jesus's name."

I bless everyone who has prayed this prayer to receive the Holy Spirit and fire in Jesus name. Fire!

CHAPTER 2

FULLY SURRENDERED

What does it look like to be completely and fully surrendered before the Lord? Not just in a moment of prayer, but in a life lived. How can we obtain surrender? Can it even be obtained?

If these are real questions you are asking yourself, I believe without a doubt you're a thirsty and hungry believer. You want more of God and everything that He has to give.

This one concept has been a constant and full reality in my life, relationship, and walk with Jesus. True surrender is birthed in gratitude. It is laying down all of our opinions and literally laying down before Him. When we get up, receiving God's opinions in his Word and allowing them to be greater than what anyone else thinks or says, even ourselves.

We desperately need to be hungry for more of God and be totally dependent upon Him in every area of our lives. He holds all things together by His Word.

"He who is satisfied loathes honey, but to the hungry soul any bitter thing is sweet" (Proverbs 27:7 AMP).

Our soul *does* thirst and hunger but there are those who say, "Oh, it's fine. I'm okay. I'm "blessed." I have a good job, a good career, a good family, and great friends and a retirement plan. I have all that one could ask for." They say, "I'm fine. I don't need anything more. I don't need more of Jesus. I have Him already. I go to church. I'm good" when God clearly says,

> *I know your works. You are neither cold nor hot. Would that you were either cold or hot! So, because you are lukewarm, and neither hot nor cold, I will spit you out of my mouth. For you say, I am rich, I have prospered, and I need nothing not realizing that you are wretched, pitiable, poor, blind and naked. I counsel you to buy from me gold refined by fire, so that you may be rich, and white garments so that you may clothe yourself and the shame of your nakedness may not be seen, and salve to anoint your eyes, so that you may see. Those whom I love, I reprove and discipline, so be zealous and repent. (Revelation 3:15–18)*

Strong words from God to the believers who are not seeking God or His will but have become satisfied with the things of this life. They use the same words as unbelievers do. They boast in their accomplishments and accolades on this earth and what the world has provided for them, all of which can be taken away at any moment. There must be a clear distinction between a believer and an unbeliever in how we *live* and *think about* this life in crises and or in increase.

Let's be a people on fire for God. Let's be a people totally in love with Jesus and abandon to His will and purposes. The heart of God burns for us to burn! He desires for us to see clearly His finished work and walk in our inheritance as children of light. We are called to be In the fire of the Holy Ghost with the light of the gospel of Jesus on our lips continually.

We are called to fear no evil but to hate what is evil and love righteousness. Let's pursue God and fellowship in the Holy Spirit with one another. We must embrace and contend for unity. It is the work of the Holy Spirit that redefines that reality in our souls.

It is easy to pull away from uncomfortable situations among one another. The world does that. This comes from either not knowing, or unbelief in, one's identity in Christ. It is a sign of pride that takes its root in insecurity which comes from fear. It is because of fear that someone would harden their heart towards a brother or sister in Christ. We are called to submit, one to another, and humble ourselves before God. Whoever finds his life will lose it, but he who loses his life for Christ's sake will find it. So then, as new creations in Christ, let's represent Jesus to the world on this earth by loving one another.

Instead of pulling away, draw closer to one another in the love of Christ. Open and vulnerable hearts build the fellowship of the family of God and allows us to abide in His peace together.

We should never speak death, even in a joking manner, to one another. We should always speak life. We should always bless one another, while approaching each other in the spirit of humility. We should also consider others greater than ourselves.

"Do nothing from selfish ambition or conceit, but in humility count others more significant than yourselves" (Philippians 2:3).

This strengthens the character of God in us and keeps us walking in love by His Spirit. Thinking and responding this way to one another will help keep us far from the deceptions of fear, pride, criticism, judgment, and personal opinions. It will encourage brotherly affection and establish sincerity in our innermost being in the love of Christ.

SEEKING THE LORD IS A LOVE AFFAIR

When you are in love with someone, there is a pursuit of one another. It is like a beautiful dance between two people who truly see one another, not for what they can get from the other but for who they are in character and in their person. At times, this dance can cause pain because parts of this dance brings more space between the two dancers than at other times when they are drawn in closer. The hands are connected, and this is the faith that they will come close again. When we are close, we can smell the hair of our beloved, we can feel their heartbeat and experience our love's touch and presence. The romance of God is a part of His glory.

You see, it's not good enough that we just play church as usual. We must be desperate for more of God. We need to seek Jesus out with all of our strength, mind, heart, soul, and spirit. He needs to be the first thing on our mind in the morning, throughout the day, and the last thing we think about before we lay down to sleep. Does He hover over your every thought, whispering, "Come, seek me out. Just be with me, I love you"? Is there a fire in you to know Him more? Do you cry out to heaven for the Spirit of wisdom and revelation in the knowledge of Him? We must seek out Jesus with everything! He is the wisdom of God. He has made Himself known through Jesus Christ, but to truly know Him, we must seek Him.

> *It is the glory of God to conceal things, but the*
> *glory of kings is to search things out. (Proverbs 25:2)*

> *Truly, you are a God who hides himself, O*
> *God of Israel, the Savior. (Isaiah 45:15)*

Desiring to be fully surrendered testifies to the inward transformation that has gone on inside of you. Ask anyone who has tasted and seen of His goodness. It's impossible to taste and see His goodness and stay the same. The very presence of God brings change. He never leaves things in the condition they once were. He is a restorer. He will restore your soul.

Jesus says, "Those who hunger and thirst after righteousness will be filled" (Matthew 5:6). Righteousness is right standing before God, to be able to stand before Him rightfully. It is the condition of being in right relationship with God. The very truth of the Gospel will compel those who know God and experience His love to surrender everything to Him. It's His goodness that brings a man's heart to repentance, not condemnation.

> *For God so loved the world that He gave His*
> *only begotten Son that whoever believes in Him will*

*not perish but have everlasting life. For God did not
send His Son into the world to condemn the world
but to give life and life more abundantly. (John
3:16–17)*

Jesus describes being fully surrendered as this:
*"If anyone wishes to come after Me, he must deny himself and take
up his cross daily and follow me" (Luke 9:23).*

Denying yourself is simple but not easy. One must lay down
personal opinions. What that looks like is not thinking so highly of
your own opinions over what the Word of God says or over anyone
in such a way that violates love, laying down wants of the flesh, which
are personal ambitions and things that bring self-gratification to you.
To deny yourself, you must be willing to lose everything to follow
Jesus. Salvation is free, but to follow Jesus will cost you everything.

There is one thing that must be removed with all prejudice to
fully surrender to God. You! Jesus calls us to live lives in Him *for*
Him, not for ourselves. We don't use God to gain things in this world
for our own pleasure. I always ask people, "So, how has your life
been in your hands?" The usual response is a really shameful, guilty
look on their faces. They look down and say, "Man, not so good."
That's because none of us were created to live for ourselves. We are
designed by Jesus to live in Him—to live a true life in holiness and
by the Spirit and power with all love and with joy. We get to lose our
lives and find Him! We get to become a living sacrifice, abounding
in the joy of the Lord and exuding the love of heaven everywhere we
go every day for Jesus, all of this while being in constant communion
and relationship with Him in the Holy Spirit. Giving up everything
that the world holds in high value to our beautiful friend, Jesus. This
is surrendering to God. Our lives belong to Him. Jesus purchased us
at the cross with His blood. Our life is not our own to disregard or
throw away. We are a people of purpose. We have a divine calling,
supreme dominion, and authority.

Get alone with God, with a sincere heart and pure motives, then
ask the Holy Spirit to reveal to you anything that you may be holding
back for yourself. Ask Him if there is any part of yourself that you

have not denied. Do that right now. Just lay it down before the Lord and ask Him to take it from you. After you do this, it's important to believe (and not question) if it "worked or not." Jesus was always telling the disciples to just "believe" and have faith. He says that if we ask anything in His name, according to His will, it will be done.

Now ask him to reveal His beauty to you. Take your time. Ask Him to show you and help you keep an open and vulnerable heart. Ask Him to show you how to contend for unity and fellowship within the church and in all your relationships.

Please pause here and consider what just happened take your time again before you continue reading.

I believe God is calling the church to a higher reality of unity and fellowship—not man-made or from human intellect but from sincere hearts by the power of the Holy Spirit to love one another. This is the command of Jesus to the church, to actually pursue and contend for unity among one another. This takes fortitude, vision, diligence, and open, gentle hearts. The kind of hearts that have been purified and tested for faith by the fire of God. It can be painful, but He prunes those He loves so they can bear more fruit. So let's contend for unity and fellowship that removes pride and arrogance. Let it destroy selfish motives while raising the standard of truth among one another. This will cause things to surface in us that the Holy Spirit will purge and purify out of us so we can look more like Jesus.

> *So now I am giving you a new commandment; love each other. Just as I have loved you, you should love each other. Your love for one another will prove to the world that you are my disciples. (John 13:34–35)*

This verse is the truth and foundation of unity. It reveals what will happen as a result of obeying this commandment. "Prove to the world" is an amazing statement. It reveals the power that is generated by us loving one another. When we love each other with the kind of love that Jesus asks us to love with, this causes power to be released. It stretches far and wide, surging in every direction. Anyone with a heartbeat notices this aroma of God's sweet goodness. It causes the world to take notice and acknowledge that we are the disciples of Christ! This is an amazing reality. God is calling the church to walk in this kind of love in Christ and for this power to be released through us by His Holy Spirit. This will shift whole nations because of the manifestation of His presence. As we surrender to intimacy with Jesus, obeying the commands of God, we will look more like Jesus and release His love and power everywhere we go!

"Philip said, 'Lord, show us the Father, and we will be satisfied'" *(John 14:8)*

Sometimes we look for something that we don't think we already have to satisfy unbelief and doubt in our hearts. We question things in our heart that the Lord has already revealed to us to be true. We ask for *more* so we can satisfy our unbelieving hearts.

"Lord, create in us a new heart that is flowing with your raging rivers of love and faith. Let peace surround our feet as we walk in obedience to your commandments. Help us, Holy Spirit, to believe the words of our Lord Jesus and desire to give Him our all. In Jesus name, Amen."

The more you surrender as a lifestyle to the Lord, the more you are consumed by His presence. His presence is always with you, but it does not always manifest. The manifest presence of Jesus is so amazing and is not always the same even for one person. For instance, I've seen His manifested presence knock people over in public. I was meeting some friends at a restaurant in Kentucky. As I was sitting there with my friends, I could not concentrate on the conversation. I kept looking around at everyone in the dining room. I saw a bunch of people with casts on their arms, shoulders in slings, and boots on their feet. I said to my friends, "I'm so sorry to leave you, but I'm going to walk around here and pray for people. They were not surprised and encouraged me as I walked away."

After praying for about five people inside, I decided to check out the patio and see who needed prayer outside. As I walked outside, I could feel the tangible presence of Jesus with me. For me, at that moment, it manifested in a sizzling-like, electric current that ran throughout my entire body in waves of glory. Then at once, a great peace and faith came over me. Suddenly, it was as if time stopped all around me as I walked. I was on heaven's time. Sometimes when the presence of Jesus manifests, it feels like time stops because Jesus doesn't live in time. In fact, He is eternity.

When I walked back inside, there was a long line of hungry college students wrapped around the room, waiting to order in front of me. I walked by this line to join my friends at our table, and my arm bumped one of these young students. At first, I didn't think anything of it, but then I heard His voice. The Lord spoke to me and simply said, "Go." That's all it took.

I quickly turned and walked toward the young lady I had bumped into. As soon as I got to her, she turned and looked up at me. That's when the Holy Spirit touched her. She suddenly collapsed and fell forward. I caught her so that she didn't hit the floor. She looked up at me in a daze. It was obvious she had no clue what was happening. She looked at me and in an intoxicated slur said, "You just smell so good." I understand how some people might have a problem with this—God supernaturally touching a young college girl in public, tells me how good I smell, then falls into a stranger's arms. Well, the Holy Spirit is free and does not live by our rules. He does whatever He wants, whenever He wants, because He is love, and there is no stopping love.

"For we are the fragrance of Christ to God among those who are being saved and among those who are perishing" (2 Corinthians 2:15).

I looked down at her and said, "That's Jesus. You just smell Jesus. Do you want that?"

She nodded her head yes. On one of the busiest days for that restaurant, in the middle of the taco line, Jesus showed up.

I looked at her friend who was with her and asked the girl, "Do you know him?"

She shook her head no as I was still holding her, her friend looking so confused you could patent the expression on her face. This young lady asked Jesus to take her life and be her Lord and Savior. She also asked Jesus to baptize her in the Holy Spirit and fill her with Himself. She immediately began sobbing and crying uncontrollably. This whole encounter was in less than a minute! This manifestation of the presence of Jesus was so amazing and so loving. He loved on His daughter that day in such a way that she will never forget and neither will the people standing by.

The Lord spoke to me one day and said, "Eman, the more you are in my presence, the more my presence will go with you and manifest around you." He spoke this to me as I was entering an Olive Garden for dinner with friends.

As we sat down to eat, I saw the waitress, and I heard in my heart that she was in aching pain all over her body. When she came over, I asked her if this was true, and she confirmed it was. I asked if I could pray for her. She looked at me and said, "Okay." After I prayed, she gasped and ran away. A few minutes later, I saw her at another table. I walked over and asked her what happened that caused her to run away so abruptly. She told me that as I was praying, all the pain had left her body.

She looked at me intently and said, "It's you!" and she dropped her water container and ran away again. I could tell she was radically encountering God's presence manifesting over her, which she had never experienced before. I went searching for her and ended up at the front reception desk to ask where she had gone. They told me she rushed into the bathroom. I waited near the reception desk to explain to her that it is Jesus who healed her. She came out, and I started to talk to her. She looked at me again and started weeping saying, "It's you, it's you" over and over.

I stopped her and reassured her, "No. That's what I came to tell you. It's Jesus. He is the one, and He is inviting you into a relationship." She accepted Jesus, and I returned to my seat.

After a while, she came over to me again and said, "I never do this, but can I have a hug?" I gave her a hug as she wept under the tangible love of God that was manifest and pouring out over her. Interestingly enough, I was with a group of young adults from church, yet when I asked the guy sitting next to me if he saw what God just did, he had no clue what had happened. If you are only focused on what's going on with you, oftentimes you can miss what God is doing in others.

I now understand from those experiences that He was speaking of His manifested presence. It is true that the righteous live by faith and not by sight but Jesus loves to manifest Himself. Those of us who know Him carry the presence of God with us. It manifests and becomes evident to those around us, although they might not know what it is they are experiencing. That's why it's our job to explain it to them. The more you are in His presence, the more His presence goes with you and will manifest around you.

"Lord may we have a fiery desire to be in Your presence and wash your feet Jesus, with our tears of thanksgiving for your blood and mercy towards us. You love us God help us to love you more and the people you put in front of us."

The glory of God is revealed when we are obedient. Obedience is the catalyst of His manifested presence. He said "Go," and I went. I have found that this kind of obedience to the Lord must be a life lived, not just once or even just for a season. As believers, we are to always be about our Father's business of going!

The first place we must go daily is a place I like to call "my mountain." Some call it the secret place or inner room. It's the "place" you go on purpose to actively be with and seek God and commune with Him and pray. I go onto the mountain of the Lord and get to minister to the Lord in the holy courts of heaven. Jesus always went onto a mountain or in a garden to talk and be with our Heavenly Father. There is something about seeking God out on purpose. It's a decision that we make to partake in His love daily. When I look at the life and ministry of Jesus, it seems that everything He did was while He was on the way to be with the Father. It's like His entire ministry followed Him as He was going to be with the Father. He spent His whole life on this earth being in His Father's presence. Oh, how the manifestation of the Father through His obedience and through the power of the Holy Spirit exploded around Jesus everywhere He went. The presence of God is what we should all desire. It's in His presence where we can "know" Jesus more and more, and this is eternal life that we know Him. (See John 17:3.) His manifested presence illuminates and permeates the spiritual and physical and saturates every molecule and structure, both in the seen and unseen. The glory of His radiance is Jesus (see Hebrews 1:3).

The Word says to seek first the kingdom of God and His righteousness. (See Matthew 6:33.) My first question to the Lord about this is, "What is your kingdom?" The term *kingdom* means a "king's domain." It is where the king abides and in which the atmosphere of His essence and nature thrives. It's the foundation of His glory. God's kingdom is His immeasurable love. We have a scripture that breaks this down even further so we can really get a better understanding.

> *For the kingdom of God is not a matter of eating and drinking but of righteousness and peace and joy in the Holy Spirit. (Romans 14:17)*

> *Nor will people say, look! Here it is! Or, see, it is there! For behold, the kingdom of God is within you[in your hearts] and among you [surrounding you]. (Luke 17:21 AMP)*

The life of Jesus on this earth perfectly models a life lived seeking first God's kingdom and righteousness. He fulfilled both and was the fulfillment of it. Jesus was anointed with the oil of joy as He was known for His joy. The Word actually says, "You have righteousness and hated lawlessness; this is why God, your God has anointed you with the oil of joy beyond your companions" (Hebrews 1:9). One thing I've learned walking with God and being filled with the Holy Spirit is that the devil hates joy. I mean he *really* hates it! There is a joy that flows from heaven (from Jesus) that is completely supernatural. It removes all cares and worries and concerns and seems to ride on the wings of faith.

Many times I have experienced this joy, and every time, there was a reaction from the enemy that tried to stifle it and remove it. The joy comes, and almost that very day the enemy comes in at every angle trying to remove me from that place of victory. He does this because he's afraid of Christians actually walking in the true joy of the Lord. He knows it's our strength. We get this strength in the joy of the Lord by our intimacy with Him. So the enemy is always at work trying to stop us from spending time with Jesus. Distractions at every turn! Have you ever noticed that when you're having a great time with Jesus, then everyone is trying to call you, telemarketers call, or someone comes knocking at your door? It takes work to get alone with Jesus and make sure we are giving Him our full attention. But it's worth it, and He is worthy of it. He wants this joy to flow into you as you spend time with Him. When you spend time with Jesus and abide in His love, you become more like Him in loving those around you especially the body of Christ.

> *If you keep My commandments [if you continue to obey My instructions], you will abide in My love and live on in it, just as I have obeyed My Father's commandments and live on in His love. I have told you these things, that My joy and delight may be in you, and that your joy and gladness may be of full measure and complete and overflowing. This is My commandment: that you love one another [Just] as I have loved you. (John 15:10–12)*

The kingdom of God is also the peace of Jesus. In the Bible, Isaiah tells us this about peace.

> *You will guard him and keep him in perfect and constant peace whose mind [both its inclination and its character] is stayed on You, because he commits himself to You, leans on You, and hopes confidently in You. So trust in the Lord [commit yourself to Him, lean on Him, hope confidently in Him] forever; for the Lord God is an everlasting Rock [the Rock of Ages]. (Isaiah 26:3–4)*

Jesus tells us this.

> *Peace I leave with you; My [own] peace I now give and bequeath to you. Not as the world gives do*

*I give to you. Do not let your hearts be troubled, nei-
ther let them be afraid. [Stop allowing yourselves to
be agitated and disturbed; and do not permit yourselves to be fearful and intimidated and cowardly
and unsettled.] (John 14:27)*

Many people do not understand that we actually have authority
to remain in the peace of Jesus. When is the last time you just sat
down and put your mind on Jesus for more than an hour? One thing
that helps with this is praying in tongues. Praying in tongues builds
us up in our most holy faith. At the same time, we are engaging the
spirit and praising Jesus by our spirit in the Holy Spirit.

I personally experience the peace of God that surpasses all
understanding every day and through many testing and trials that
don't feel good in the natural, but my heart will remain at peace like
still waters. Without getting into too much detail, I was in jail one
time shortly after I left a really amazing prayer conference. I did not
want to be in jail and was not very happy about my situation. Laying
down on my cot the first night, I told the Lord, "I really don't want
to be here."

He said to me, "This is your promotion." Now, in the natural
world that made no sense. How could me being in jail be a promotion? Stories began to flood my mind. One in particular was Joseph
who was sold into slavery by his brothers, which ended up being the
plan for him becoming the secondhand man to Pharaoh and ruler
of the entire modern world at that time. That's quite the promotion
although I'm sure while he was sitting in jail he did not think so.

There I was, thinking about Joseph as I was laying in jail. Then
I realized, "I may never get this opportunity again to praise God
in this kind of trial and circumstance." So I began to worship God
right there in the middle of the jail room with dozens of inmates and
guards all around. I worshipped like I would if no one was there.
Then, the manifest peace and presence of Jesus filled me, then filled
the entire jail house so much so that the inmates up top who were on
suicide watch were so silent that the guards noticed and made com-
ments about how peaceful and well-behaved everyone seemed to be.

It was not common and was noticed by many of the inmates. The "cell boss" or leader of the other inmates approached me one day. He said, "I've been watching you ever since you got here. You have this peace on you and everyone can see it and they want it. It's like you don't have a care in the world." So I told him about Jesus, and he repented for murders that he committed and was never caught for. He released and forgave himself. He cried then turned and prayed for me. If you can't receive prayer from a murderer, you may not be as humble as you might think you are.

That same day, God spoke to me and told me to give my dinner to one of the inmates they called "preacher" because he was always reading the Bible to people. I gave him my meal, and he invited me to sit down. He told me he had been praying for revival in that place for years. He showed me in the back of his Bible his prayer for God to send him someone to help him minister. That's when I knew why God had me there. I told him that I was a minister and did power evangelism, simply meaning that I demonstrated the power of God to people I was sharing Jesus with. I thanked him for praying me into jail with a laugh and asked him to follow me. I gave him a crash course in evangelism as we walked around the jail praying for people and shared the gospel. Over a dozen people gave their lives to Jesus. Two were baptized in the sinks (one in that jail and another in the next jail they transferred me to). Many people were physically healed, and many demons were cast out of people. It was a revival!

When we look at the life of Jesus and how He lived, one thing is strongly evident: Jesus lived a life fully surrendered, making Him passionately obedient to the will of God because He loved His Father. Obedience is also a display of love. Jesus said, "If anyone loves me, he will obey my word"(John 14:23). Are you willing to do and go anywhere for Jesus? Even into a prison or third world country or maybe in the business world? Are you willing to go and do anything and boldly proclaim the name of Jesus? If you are, He will send you and speak to you. Will you be obedient? Will you say yes to Jesus no matter how difficult what He may be telling you to do is?

PRAYER

Jesus, make us a people of surrender every day. Keep us in your everlasting presence so that we may walk in the manifestation of your presence everywhere we go, releasing your fragrance in the darkest of places to those who will be saved and to the perishing. Let us see the hearts, minds, and souls of those around us anywhere we are come to life in you by the power of the Holy Spirit. Lead us into all obedience so that our only answer to your voice is "Yes!" We will shine like the sons and daughters you have made us to be, looking just like you, Lord—looking like love on this earth as it is in heaven. Let it be on us. Amen.

CHAPTER 3

FOLLOW HIM

Salvation is a free gift of faith but to follow
Jesus will cost you everything.

The great love of our Heavenly Father is bigger than your unbelief. It is bigger than your fear, bigger than worries, and bigger than your comfort zones. His love is bigger than your sin, bigger than any lie we could possibly believe. Creation itself leaves us without excuse to believe in the great power and beauty of God, the Creator of all (see Romans 1:20)! Likewise, the crucifixion of Jesus leaves us without excuse of the love of God for us by giving His only son to be beaten beyond description and marred more than any son of man. He was brutally murdered on a tree to become sin, yet was blameless of any sin. He became sin for the sake of the world to rescue those who would believe. This was Jesus following the will of the Father. God's will was that Jesus would be obedient to the point of death, only to rise again on the third day as was prophesied by Christ Himself. Jesus asks of us a similar journey of obedience. He asks us to deny ourselves, pick up our cross, and follow Him (see Matthew 16:24–25). It cost Jesus His life. We know that no servant is greater than his master. If it happened to Jesus, it will happen to us. That's precisely why Jesus tells us that we must lose our lives for His sake to find it. That's the cost to follow Jesus—your life.

Jesus spent His entire life on earth following the Father in every way. He spent more time with the Father than anyone ever has.

Salvation is free but to follow Jesus costs everything. When God called me, I was holding onto my life with a fearfully tight grip. I was a single father and never expected God to do what He did. I remember I was mowing the lawn when I heard the Lord speak to me over the mower. He said, "Are you willing to lose your daughter for me?"

Those words shot through me like lightning. I was completely shocked at this question. I immediately stopped everything I was doing. The question still ringing throughout every part of my being, I said, "What do you mean?" No response, but I knew it was not a rhetorical question. He asked me, and He wanted an answer. I said to the Lord, "Yes."

As a father, I was thinking of the worst-case scenario. I immediately thought that something bad was going to happen to her. I didn't know what was going to happen. That summer, for the first time, I let my daughter stay with her grandparents on her mom's side. I assumed this must be what He meant (I was hoping). The day that my daughter came back from summer break was the same day that we had to leave the house that we lived in. I had no place to go except the van with our belongings in it. We were homeless. That first night, I remember thinking I should stay with my sister for a few nights until I could work some things out. On my way, the Holy Spirit said, "Don't stay more than four days." So I obeyed the Lord and didn't stay for more than four days.

On the last night at my sister's, I had a vision from the Lord in the middle of the night. In the vision, as crystal clear as the best 4G TV, I was walking in a desert talking to foreign people. I knew that I had great favor from this man and his family. When we stopped and I was leaving the man and his family, he spoke to me and said, "You are welcome in Bollywood anytime" in a thick, Indian accent. At that very moment, I was caught up in the air and was traveling across the earth over India. As I came over a large city crowded with people, it seemed like everyone was wearing yellow. I stopped over the most beautiful courtyard with trees just budding and almost in bloom.

As I descended into the courtyard, at the front was a building five stories high, shaped like a V, with two roads along each side. At the very entrance of this interesting building was a brilliantly red, giant door. It was so beautiful that I had to go inside. After visiting inside, I walked across the street to a house and was greeted by an old man who asked me, "Son do you need a ride home?"

I said, "Yes, I do."

He walked me to this huge old mobile boat of a car. I got in the backseat. As we were driving, the old man had a seizure or a heart attack and died as he was driving me home. I was panicked because he died, and no one was driving the car.

Right then, an old man with a white beard appeared out of thin air right next to me, looked at me with a smile, and said, "Oh, don't worry." Then he jumped into the driver's seat and began driving after moving the other man out of the way. I was very alarmed to say the least. This man was so jolly and happy. He looked at me in the rear mirror and said with a smile, "Hey! Do you need me to pray for you?"

I said, "Yes! I do!" So the old guy reached back with one hand on the wheel and stuck his finger in my left ear and began to pray for me. I thought to myself, *This is so strange*. Right then, I woke up out of the encounter, but as I awoke, I could still feel the finger in my left ear for a good three to four minutes.

The Holy Spirit spoke to me and said, "Listen." He had my attention. How could I forget the encounter, anyway? It was so real, as if it had really happened. That morning was the last day at my sister's house. I packed my daughter and I up, and as I was driving away, I heard the Lord speak to me and say, "I want you to release the care of your daughter to your mother." Now this was starting to feel like too much. Everything in me wanted to say, "*No* way!" but I drove over to my mother's house. I was not very close to my mom at that time, so I was not content with this.

As I entered my mother's house, I watched my mom suddenly have a mother's heart toward my daughter, which surprised me. That's when my mom said, "You need to let me keep her."

Every part of me was screaming, "No! She is mine. I won't." Right then, I heard the voice of the Lord just simply say my name. I knew it was God's plan that he warned me about before all of this happened. He asked me if I was willing to lose my daughter for Him. I reluctantly said yes. After a few days, I had her school bus schedule changed to my mother's house.

I decided I needed to let my daughter's mom know she was going to be living with my mom while I didn't have a home. I texted her and told her the news. I was not prepared for her response. She said, "Have you thought about missions?"

I was shocked. I responded, "What are you talking about?"

She said, "I was praying for peace concerning our daughter, and I saw you walking in a desert talking to foreign people." She went on to tell me that this vision confused her because she was not even thinking about me, then saw the word *missions* come across the vision God was showing her. She said, "I think you're supposed to be a missionary. Actually, I know you are supposed to be a missionary."

I was floored. Here it was just the next day after my open night vision where the Lord was showing me walking in a desert talking to foreign people in missions and now this from my ex-wife. I mean, this was the woman who left me for my older brother. How could the Lord use her to confirm His Word to me? It was the least likely place of confirmation for me but actually the perfect place. God definitely knows how to keep us humble. I was beside myself.

In the days to come, it was very hard for me to let go and trust God in what He was calling me into. It felt like I had lost everything, Yet I had a peace and confidence in this love that God had poured into my heart that made it true to me. Even though my circumstances seemed like the worst, I didn't feel as though anything had changed in me for the worst. It was like God let everything that was an idol in my life be stripped away, and the only thing I could do was trust God. If He didn't show up every day, I would be lost.

I remember the first night without a roof over my head. It was the cold season, so I went into a Kroger grocery store to use their bathroom. However, the real reason was to go someplace warm where I could weep. It was a single bathroom with a deadbolt lock. I locked the door behind me and immediately began to weep before the Lord. After an hour or so, I got up off the floor and looked at myself in the mirror. I was a mess. The reality of my natural circumstance was surely present and the weight of it very real. I looked at myself in the eyes, bloodshot from crying so hard all night. As I looked into my own eyes, suddenly I saw something in myself. It flashed for a moment. It was like I wasn't looking at myself anymore. It was like a lion was inside of me and was staring back at me. I could feel its power and authority. I had never seen anything like it before. Then I could feel the Lord's presence and peace like I cannot explain come over me. After this, the Lord began to send me out on the streets to share the Gospel with anyone and everyone. He flew me all over the United States of America one way, no reservations. I saw hundreds and hundreds of salvations. Baptisms, healings, and miracles followed me everywhere the Lord sent me—most of which no one knew about. Most things He did, no one still knows about except Jesus and me. I had been thrust into the harvest!

We must believe the Father is with us, with all confidence and assurance in our hearts of His great love for us. It is impossible to please God without faith. Everything that God asks of us or is about requires faith. Forgiveness, for example, is something God commands us to do with everyone including ourselves. So what does forgiveness look like by faith? When we forgive someone, we speak it out loud. We speak life. "I forgive you." It's important to realize and remember we don't live by sight but by faith. When we forgive, we need to realize it doesn't matter what we are feeling in the moment. Jesus said what comes out of a man's mouth comes out of his heart. What we speak determines the true position of our heart, not what we are feeling. If you can speak, "I forgive you," then you *do* forgive no matter how you may *feel* about it. This is where faith is the key. We must believe that we forgive despite our feelings. This pleases God. Our feelings will eventually line up with the truth, but our feelings are never to dictate the true position of our hearts.

People who don't understand this get caught up in the lie of unbelief concerning forgiveness. This keeps people in a constant place of questioning their hearts because they don't "feel" like they forgave. They allow emotion to lead and dictate the position of their heart when it's what is *spoken* that reveals the heart. People feel like they constantly need "inner healing" because the enemy stirs up some emotions concerning someone they said they forgave and because of the lack of knowledge of how faith applied to forgiveness works. They believe the emotional lie over the truth of life that was spoken from their hearts. Believe! You will live by faith and not emotions. Emotions are not bad, but if we live by them, we will ride a constant up and down life of discouragement only as good as others allow us to be. That is not the abundant life that Jesus paid for us to have. Trust that what comes out of your mouth is what your heart is saying. So speak life and activate forgiveness by believing you forgave. This kind of faith pleases God and will keep you walking in the spirit of faith. What we say is more important than what we feel, but nothing can ever speak louder than Jesus's blood over our lives.

Pray this prayer of forgiveness with me for anyone you may need to forgive, even if it's yourself. "Lord I forgive ___, and I bless them in your name that they may know your love. I also forgive myself Lord for not loving how you created me to love, help me to be more like you Jesus. Thank you Lord that you are changing me and making me shine more and more like you, in Jesus's name, Amen.

CHAPTER 4

THE LANGUAGE OF FAITH

The words of God are life. Jesus is the one and only life giving spirit. First Corinthians 15:45 says that God spoke the world into existence by faith through Himself. He spoke, and something that was not then came into existence. God is love and that love speaks by faith. Faith working through love formed the universe. He dressed it with His glory and crowned it with His likeness. A battle constantly rages and wars against us because of the deception of Satan. Unbelief has become the ruler in this world.

We've all been born into sin and born into unbelief. People are schooled in unbelief and have doctorates in doubt. Doubt comes as easily off their lips as fear flows from their hearts. This is the reality that most of us were born into. We are taught not to get our hopes up because the world will let us down. People train children out of their own disappointments and failures. However, when we look at the Bible and how Jesus treated people, we see a new way.

Having faith in God is the lesson to the clambering disciples that Jesus taught. Position yourself in Him and trust. Believe who He says you are and have confidence in Him. Give Him your whole life and have assurance that you will be with Him in heaven and that He will be with you always. Jesus, our stability, has come into the world, and He desires to move into our hearts. By communing with Him, His Word will stifle unbelief and release the power hidden in His hands. Those same nail-torn hands that formed the world as He was slain for before the foundation of the world. That same power that was hidden in his hands is in our hands and feet. As we were crucified *with* Him in death that we may also be raised with Him in glory and power.

> *And His brightness was as the light; He had horns coming out of His hand: and there was the diding of His power. (Habakkuk 3:4 KJV)*

> *I have been crucified with Christ [In Him I have shared His crucifixion]; it is no longer I who live, but Christ [the Messiah] lives in me and the life I now live in the body I live by faith in [by adherence to and reliance on and complete trust in] the Son of God, who loved me and gave Himself up for me. (Galatians 2:20 AMPC)*

> *For if we have become one with Him by sharing a death like His, we shall also be [one with Him in sharing] His resurrection [by a new life lived for God]. (Romans 6:5 AMPC)*

We must believe that we are the hands and feet of Jesus on the earth right now. We must understand that we all have work to do for God, and He desires for us to fulfill that ministry. There is power hidden in our hands! Jesus paid for it and wants us to release it everywhere we go. He has prepared our feet with the gospel of peace because of the nail that was driven into His feet so that we could walk in His peace.

"Give us faith in you Jesus and in your Word that we are your children and walk with you in faith in all confidence trusting in you by the power of the Holy Spirit."

Paul writes in 1 Corinthians 13:13,

> *These three things remain, faith, hope and love but the greatest of these is love.*

Now faith is the assurance of things hoped for and the evidence of things not yet seen. (Hebrews 11:1)

When I look further at what Paul is saying and what the Lord is saying, it takes on a greater meaning and a vital truth about the reality that surrounds us.

Fight the good fight of the faith. Take hold of the eternal life to which you were called and about which you made the good confession in the presence of many witnesses. (1 Timothy 6:12)

The fight is no longer against sin because the law of sin and death was defeated on the cross.

There is therefore now no condemnation for those who are in Christ Jesus. For the law of the Spirit of life has set you free in Christ Jesus from the law of sin and death. For God has done what the law, weakened by the flesh, could not do. By sending His own Son in the likeness of sinful flesh and for sin, He condemned sin in the flesh, in order that the righteous requirement of the law might be fulfilled in us, who walk not according to the flesh but according to the Spirit. For those who live according to the flesh set their minds on the things of the flesh, but those who live according to the Spirit set their minds on the things of the Spirit. For to set the mind on the flesh is death, but to set the mind on the Spirit is life and peace. For the mind that is set on the flesh is hostile to God, for it does not submit to God's law; indeed, it cannot. Those who are in the flesh cannot please God. You, however, are not in the flesh but in the Spirit, if in fact the Spirit of God dwells in you. Anyone who does not have the Spirit of Christ does not belong to him. But if Christ is in you, although the body is dead because of sin, the Spirit is life because of righteousness. If the Spirit of him who raised Jesus from the dead dwells in you, he who raised Christ Jesus from the dead will also give life to your mortal bodies through his Spirit who dwells in you. (Romans 8:1–10)

The key here is those in the flesh cannot please God. In other words, if faith is what pleases God, for those born of this world who live in unbelief, it is impossible for them to please God because they do not have faith in God.

This is very good news! we who are in Christ are free! But notice in this passage of truth, there is a key to knowing if we are living according to the flesh or according to the Spirit. It is what we set our minds on. If we set our minds on the troubles of this world or on the things that we think we need to acquire, then we are walking according to the flesh. For instance, the material gain in building oneself up in this lifetime for monetary success or for the recognition of this world. Another example would be for the praise of man. When we set our minds on the things of this world, we have no life in us. But as believers, we are compelled by the Holy Spirit to set our minds on the Spirit, giving us life and peace. The glorious peace of the Lord and the unshakable assurance of His presence and truth becomes manifested.

Everyone is trying to achieve peace and wants to be loved. They just don't know that they already *are* loved or if they *did* know, they forgot. Peace is so amazing and is one of my favorite manifestations of the Holy Spirit. It positions our hearts, minds, and spirits to receive our Father's love. This enables the power of the Holy Spirit to be greater than any circumstance or situation we may face. This means we remain victorious in Christ, seated with Him in heavenly places, experiencing on earth the victory that He has already won. As we walk with the Holy Spirit, we will walk more and more in this reality. It will grow deep within us, as we believe the revelation of

God's great mystery—"Jesus, the hope of glory, living with us!" (see Colossians 1:27).

Jesus is the Prince of Peace because He abides in the Father. The reality of who the Father is to Jesus and who Jesus is as his Son is the reality of truth itself. When Jesus walked this earth before He was glorified, He was with His Father every day and His love manifested every day. Jesus was always assured of who He was in His true identity as the Son of the Living God.

Jesus's faith in who He was, the Son of the Living God, is without question the greatest portion of faith that has ever walked on this earth. This leads us to examine ourselves, not to criticize or condemn ourselves but to look to the hope that is in us. That the same faith that belongs to Jesus also belongs to us because He gave it to us. He said, "Everything that belongs to me, I give them." We have all the faith we need to literally move mountains (see 2 Peter 1:3)! This assurance is embodied in the truth and reality of our identity as sons and daughters in His kingdom. We are filled with the fullness of Christ and we are the righteousness of God in Christ Jesus (see 2 Corinthians 5:21).

When Jesus said, "Satan, get behind me," Satan got behind Jesus and has been behind Him ever since. What the Lord declares is established. Nowhere in the Gospels do we hear the disciples tell Satan to get behind them. They knew he was already behind them. Jesus says to submit to God, resist the devil, and he will flee. He didn't say to reason with him, and he will flee. He is already behind you! Resisting him is simply submitting to God and giving thanks, supplications, and declarations to the Lord for who He is. We are glorious sons and daughters of the king, righteous and holy, of a royal priesthood, seated in heavenly places, blessed with every spiritual blessing, given all authority and power to reign in this life and the one to come, free from offense, worry, doubt, anger, bitterness, fear, and jealousy and *bold* before the throne of grace. You have all peace and confidence that God is good and faithful and has transformed us with a new mind—the mind of Christ.

"Thank you, Lord, for these things. Thank you for helping us submit to you as the devil flees before your holy presence, reminded of his defeat because we are covered in your blood. So we worship you Lord of heaven and earth. In Jesus's name, Amen."

The one and only king Jesus is victorious over the enemy. He is confident in His finished work. The Holy Spirit has come and is the greatest gift that the world has ever known. Would you charge your children for a gift you wanted to give them? Never! Neither has our Heavenly Father charged us a price for the greatest gift of eternity. The Holy Spirit has been given to us freely and made available to us by faith in the precious blood of our Lord, Jesus.

The grace of God crushes the oppression of the enemy. It crushes the law of sin and death. We must put on the love of Christ. There is nothing that we cannot do when the Lord Jesus is with us. What can stand against us? Who can stand against us? We belong to Christ, and God's will is that we would stand in faith. He wants us to stand in His presence as the prophets of old—standing before Him righteous and holy by His Son, Jesus. Standing blameless, without shame and without guilt. This is available to us in Jesus because He is the way to the Father, and He has purchased all the junk He does not want us to have. He paid for our freedom to be blameless before Him!

Once, I was standing before the Lord with my hands lifted during worship at a church. A strange thing occurred that day. I was just so happy to worship my king and didn't care what it looked like or what anyone thought of my worship. To me, it was just me and my beautiful friend, Jesus. I was in the front as the worship team lifted up His name. Right then, I felt a fist-sized knot raise up in my back, and it began to throb in pain.

Suddenly I heard the voice of the Lord, Jesus, speak to me. He said, "Oh, don't worry about that. Go over there in the aisle and lay down, and I will walk on your back and take it right out."

I hesitated. What a strange thing to hear from Jesus. Though it was so clear, even more clear than I've ever heard Him speak to me before that moment, I was surprised at the command. In all my hesitation, He spoke again, "Go ahead! Go, go!" His tone was very joyful and encouraging as if I were a toddler who needed encouragement with gentle love taps on my diaper.

I went as the Lord instructed me to. I walked over where I had envisioned Him telling me to go. I did as the Lord instructed, but I laid down just behind the guest speaker. I know the Lord honors obedience because the next moment I could feel these large rings coming from above and crashing down over me and expanding outward. There were two of them, one right after the other, much like the rings in the movie *Star Gate* that came down to teleport the person in the circles onto the mothership. The knot was completely gone out of my back! I was beside myself in His presence, in awe of the power of God.

I got up from the floor and walked back to my seat to worship God. With holy hands lifted high, I worshipped God singing in tongues. After a few minutes of worshipping in tongues, I felt this great faith come over me. It was as though I had the faith to lift off the floor right then and there and fly up into the air. Lightness came over me. I believed I was going to lift off the ground.

Overwhelmed with this faith and lightness, I noticed someone's hand on my back, on the bottom part of my left shoulder blade. It was very warm and gentle as I rocked back and forth in the presence of my Father. I thought to myself, *Wow, someone is really loving me right now.* I deliberated for a moment thinking about who it might be praying for me with their hand on my back. That's when Jesus interrupted my inner dialogue and said, "Go ahead and look." So I turned to see whose hand was on my back praying for me. To my amazement, there was no one there. The hand was still there touching my back!

I looked ahead and thought, *What is going on?* So I asked Jesus, "Is that you Lord?"

He said, "No, it's one of my angels." As soon as He said that, an angel appeared next to me on the left. He stood over twelve feet tall. All I could see was what looked like a column of brilliantly white fluffy feathers. He ruffled his feathers very jubilantly, and the sound of the ruffling of the feathers was so loud and intense it drowned out the music coming from the worship team.

As he ruffled his feathers, a wind hit my face. I suppose He was taking off to fly because the next thing I knew, I was not standing in the church anymore. I was in another place. The first thing I noticed was that in this place, time didn't exist. The sheer raw power of God permeated and saturated the fabric of everything. It was like the power of God in this place was the greatest reality I'd ever known. It was jarring and fearful, the power of the Most High. I looked to my left, and I could see the angel next to me, standing in full majesty. I looked forward, and I was standing inside of a bright blue, misty light. Although I couldn't sense it, there was actually something under my feet that I was standing on—a blue light that was so beautiful. Within that blue light was white light shooting all around very fast. The white light within the blue light was active and alive, *excited* with life. I looked to my right, and there was another angel that I hadn't noticed until then, but his details were hidden to me. Also to my right was a large throne, though I could not see anyone on it. I knew God was on the throne, though He is invisible. I looked again through the bright blue misty light, and I could see a city in the distance.

This all was so overwhelming, and I began to think to myself that I shouldn't be here. Fear began to grip me because of the majesty of His presence and splendor. It was like the atmosphere was royalty. Before the fear totally overwhelmed me, I saw a giant circle of angels and sons and daughters of God fully in their majesty and glory, and I was a part of this family of heaven! Then a knowing from the Lord ministered to my heart and said, "You don't deserve to be here, but you have been adopted into the majesty of the royal family of God. You are accepted." My being was flooded with the power and love of God. In the presence of God, rejection and wrong thinking left, and He reassured me of the truth. I was in heaven and was included in the royal family of God because of the blood of Jesus. Nothing and no one can change that.

I don't remember coming back, but I did come back and had a sense that I could have seen more and received more had I not let fear in or began to try and intellectualize or overthink what God was doing. I think that's a good lesson for us who tend to overthink and analyze everything. God is far above our minds and knowledge, and it's prideful to think we can analyze and comprehend the fullness and glory of God. We can just trust Him, enjoy His presence, and allow Him to reveal and show us what He wants, whenever He wants.

Let's take a moment for prayer. I would like to pray for childlike faith and encounters in the heavenly realm. If you have ever wanted angelic visitations or a heavenly encounter with the Lord, pray this prayer with me.

"Lord Jesus, help me to be so childlike that I can believe anything is possible. Help me to truly see you with joy and awe. Open my eyes to see the angels you have surrounded me with. Fill me with faith to go higher into the heavenly realms of your glory and majesty. Lord, remove all doubt and fear from my heart. Destroy every lying spirit on me right now keeping me from encountering you. In Jesus's name. Amen."

CHAPTER 5

REST

It is God's will and desire that we will enter into His
eternal rest. The world is not at rest but God is.

The rest of God is a place that our hearts enter into, our soul abides
in, and our spirit rejoices in. God is calling those who would believe
in Him into this eternal rest...where the circumstances and resis-
tances in this world have no effect on our hearts and souls. It is a
permanent home for us to reside in, commune with Him, and know
Him. If you listen carefully enough you can hear the rest of God calling your name, "Come. Come sit with Me and be with Me." You can
hear the song of the Lord singing over you and inviting you into His
rest. The blood of Jesus has made a way for us to enter into this place.
We can drink the blood of Jesus and enjoy the rest of God. He has
accomplished and finished His work. We must believe it is accomplished and have a revelation of the power of the blood of Jesus. Only
by faith can we enter into the rest of God.

> *For only we who believe can enter His rest,*
> *as for the others, God said, "In my anger I took an*
> *oath: 'They will never enter My place of rest.'" Even*
> *though this rest has been ready since He made the*
> *world. (Hebrews 4:3)*

Therefore, while the promise of entering his rest still stands. Let us fear lest any of you should seem to have failed to reach it. For good news came to us just as to them, but the message they heard did not benefit them, because they were not united by faith with those who listened. For we who have believed enter that rest, as he has said. (Hebrews 4:1–3)

Let us therefore strive to enter that rest, so that no one may fall by the same sort of disobedience, For the word of God is living and active, sharper than any two-edged sword, piercing to the division of soul and of spirit, of joints and of marrow, and discerning the thoughts and intentions of the heart. And no creature is hidden from his sight, but all are naked and exposed to the eyes of him whom we must give account. (Hebrews 4:11)

What does it mean to strive to enter the rest of God? He is talking about the spiritual discipline that one must have to believe. People say, "Oh, brother, I believe." Yet when the trial comes to test their faith, they quickly lose their faith and peace goes out the window. They allow circumstances to determine their reality instead of what God has spoken in His Word. It takes spiritual discipline to pass the trials that come to test our faith (see 1 Peter 1:7). It's time we get passionate about God and His Word! Praying in the Holy Ghost builds us up in our most holy faith. Worshipping Jesus not *just* in a worship service but when no one is looking except Him. In the secret place, let's lift up our holy hands before the Lord because He is worthy. Let's have a hunger for His Word and meditate on it every day. With fasting and praying, let's wash the feet of Jesus with our tears of thankfulness for His blood which has washed us of our sins. His great love has made a way for us to be children of God. He is worthy of all praise. All of our worship and prayer and praise and honor to Jesus is for only one reason. There must only be one motive. He is worthy!

We have to lose our entitlement and our opinions! We deserve death but Jesus came. It's all for Him and by Him.

PRAYER

"Lord, may we glorify you and praise you! You are worthy of it all! Show us a thankful heart within us. Empower us to enter into your rest by faith. Give us a fire to give you all of our attention. In Jesus's name."

Everything is better in God's rest. Just lean in on Jesus and leave your cares and concerns behind. Lean into Him! It takes faith to enter in. We must build ourselves up in our most holy faith by praying in the Holy Spirit. Ask Jesus to help any unbelief you may have. We need Him to help us because we can do nothing apart from Him.

In the place of God's eternal rest, we bear fruit that remains, and there is growth that is accelerated in the spirit. It's also the place where the river of joy, love, and faith flow from. I don't want to be on the shore of the river waiting for a splash from a crash on the rocks. I want to roll over into that river and be carried away into the heart of my Heavenly Father! I want full submersion in the river of God. I want to know His love and know Him. I want to receive the fullness of His love for me and be who He has created me to be since the foundation of the world. A beloved son and friend of God—fully received, fully loved, fully accepted, and never rejected or abandoned. We are completely blessed by our Heavenly Father by His finished work on the cross through Jesus. May we rest from every concern and care of the world and be with our king, Jesus, abiding in Him as He abides in the Father.

Ultimately God wants us to receive the love He has for us. Think about being in love with someone and you so long and desire for them to receive the love you have for them, but there is a block in them that's stopping the flow of your love. They don't know how to receive the kind of love you have for them. They may even want to be in a position to receive it, but they don't know or fully understand who they are to you. Their hearts are open to it and willing but work needs to be done for them to fully receive the love you have for them. It's always vulnerability that opens intimacy to be known by someone. Adam and Eve sinned, hid from God, and covered themselves. They were fully known by God until they separated themselves by sin (lack of trust). So they covered their intimacy from God, and that's what really stops us from knowing Him. It is a lack of intimacy with the Father.

His love is like a vast ocean—so deep that you can't know the depths or swim to the bottom of it without losing your own life. That's the cost of His love. You cannot swim to the bottom of the ocean in your own power. At some point, you would be crushed by the weight of His glory in the depths of His love. Then you will be carried away to the bottom by the power that surrounds you. One must lose his life to find it, and then you will begin to truly know the depths of His love. You can't get there on your own. What are your muscles, your bones, your mind, or your strength? The helper is here. Let Him help! He is mighty. Stop struggling. Die to your own efforts and ability, and let Him love you. You're worth being loved.

"God help us believe the truth and trust you with confidence that sets us free from the lies of this world and free from our own selves. Help us be vulnerable with you and fully known by you. Help us to be intimate and honest with you while we draw close to you, Father. In Jesus's name. Amen."

CHAPTER 6

THE SPIRIT OF FORGIVENESS

Condemnation of any kind is a lie for those who are in Christ (see Romans 8). Do not allow lies that people believe and speak against you to cause any condemnation in you. Likewise, do not speak in any way against someone that would make room for the enemy to condemn anyone else. God is kind, and He has called us to be kind to one another. There is room in that kindness for rebuke and correction. Kindness is a position of the heart that always rests on peace. We must always remember that truth is what sets people free and the Holy Spirit is the one who convicts. Jesus has spoken all that needs to be said concerning what is truth. Keep close to the words of our Lord.

Love keeps no record of wrongs. This is only possible to walk in by the Holy Spirit working within us. The power of the Holy Spirit enables us to walk in this love. He says in Hebrews 8:12, "For I will be merciful to their unrighteousness, and their sins and their iniquities will I remember no more." We must forget people's wrongs against us. This is true forgiveness, which is love. Jesus said in Mark 11:26, "But if you don't forgive, neither will the Father in heaven forgive your wrongdoing." This is a shocking reality. Jesus puts the highest possible weight and penalty on forgiveness.

In Matthew 18:21–35, Jesus speaks to Peter about the importance of forgiveness and the penalty of unforgiveness.

Then Peter came up and said to him, "Lord, how often will my brother sin against me, and I forgive him? As many as seven times?" Jesus said to him, "I do not say to you seven times, but seventy-seven times.

"Therefore the kingdom of heaven may be compared to a king who wished to settle accounts with his servants. When he began to settle, one was brought to him who owed him ten thousand talents. And since he could not pay, his master ordered him to be sold, with his wife and children and all that he had, and payment to be made.

So the servant fell on his knees, imploring him, 'Have patience with me, and I will pay you everything.'

And out of pity for him, the master of that servant released him and forgave him the debt. But when that same servant went out, he found one of his fellow servants who owed him a hundred denarii, and seizing him, he began to choke him, saying, 'Pay what you owe.'

So his fellow servant fell down and pleaded with him, 'Have patience with me, and I will pay you.' He refused and went and put him in prison until he should pay the debt. When his fellow servants saw what had taken place, they were greatly distressed, and they went and reported to their master all that had taken place.

Then his master summoned him and said to him, 'You wicked servant! I forgave you all that debt because you pleaded with me. And should not you have had mercy on your fellow servant, as I had mercy on you?' And in anger his master delivered him to the jailers, until he should pay all his debt. So also my heavenly Father will do to every one of you, If you do not forgive your brother from your heart." (Matthew 18:21–35)

Jesus even modeled forgiveness in the Lord's prayer when His disciples asked Him how they should pray.

> *Pray then like this:*
> *"Our Father in heaven, hallowed be your name, Your kingdom come, your will be done, on earth as it is in heaven.*
> *Give us this day our daily bread, and forgive us our debts, as we also have forgiven our debtors.*
> *And lead us not into temptation but deliver us from evil." (Matthew 6:9–13)*

He clearly tells us to forgive just as the Father forgives us. Jesus even goes so far as to say this,

> *For if you forgive others their trespasses, your heavenly Father will also forgive you, but if you do not forgive others their trespasses, neither will your Father forgive your trespasses. (Matthew 6:14–15 ESV)*

God is very serious about forgiveness. If you are keeping a list of the wrongs a person has done to you, you are in violation of God's law of love. You are operating in unforgiveness.

Forgiveness in the Greek actually means "pardoned." When a prisoner is pardoned by the president of the United States, for instance, He is forgiven for his error or offense. God takes it further and erases your transgressions away by the blood of Jesus. God is asking us to forgive others as He does and remember their sins against them no more. God's law is love—to keep no record of wrongs against people when we forgive someone. We are all commanded by God to love one another. That is why it says,

> *Therefore, my beloved, as you have always obeyed, so now, not only as in my presence but much more in my absence, work out your own salvation with fear and trembling, for it is God who works in*

you, both to will and to work for His good pleasure.
(Philippians 2:12 ESV)

This is done through a day-by-day walk with Jesus. If you don't live in the present with Jesus, you will always feel like you're incomplete. God wants to forgive you. That's why He gave His Son Jesus to pour out His blood and affection for you. He made a way for all of us to be free from ourselves and the lies of the enemy. If we don't let Him do this, we won't make it. If we don't love, we won't make it. If we don't forgive, we won't be forgiven.

There is hope. His name is Jesus. If you believe in Him and confess Him as Lord, He will live in you, and He is mighty to save! Let Jesus have His perfect work in you. The world says, "I'll forgive, but I'll never forget." This kind of thinking leads to death. It is the wisdom of the world but not the wisdom of God. God commands us to forgive one another and keep no record of a suffered wrong against anyone.

"Bearing with one another and, If one has a complaint against another, forgiving each other; as the Lord has forgiven you, so you also must forgive" (Colossians 3:13).

This means not counting it against someone anymore and never bringing it up to slight or condemn them. That will cast a shadow over them to others which encourages judgment and criticism, directly opposing the law and command to love one another. People who get trapped in this become very near sighted and never see clearly enough to change the world around them with Jesus who lives in them.

THE SHAKING

The concrete floor was cold and hard. The air was like breathing in thick mouthfuls of despair and hopelessness. Boisterous voices filled with depression masked by fragile mocking laughter reverberated off the concrete walls. I could feel all of my bones laying on that floor. Hope seemed like a flicker of light that had fallen down a dark tunnel of shadows.

Disoriented and gripped by fear, I lay on the concrete floor listening as criminals act as lawyers going over one another's cases and offering up legal counsel to each other. The holding cell was overcrowded. Everything revolved around a guard coming in and out to give whatever announcement came next.

I was not expecting to be in a jail cell the morning I was supposed to go to family court. Just the night before this happened, I had a dream. In the dream, I was going up an escalator, and when I got to the top, I was surrounded by demons. On my left, there was a presence of someone standing next to me. The demons were closing in on me, and I could see they had a table prepared to lay me on. Just then the leader of these demons walked through. Slowly, they all parted and made way for her. She was tall and wearing a dirty purple dress. Her eyes were dark and full of hate.

I stepped up to her and began to sing a song, "To Him who sits on the throne and unto the Lamb, be blessings and honor and glory and power, forever." I sang it over and over and over.

The demons began to scream and cover their ears and fall to the ground, rolling and crawling away. The face of the leader of the demons turned to boiling anger and hatred. She knew she could not hold me there or chain me to that table.

I turned around and slid down the stairs onto the sidewalk. That's when I noticed I actually had one angel on each side, behind me. Then the lady demon appeared in front of me outside, and I spoke the song one more time right in her face, "To Him who sits on the throne and unto the Lamb, be blessings and honor and glory and power forever and ever." She disappeared, and then I woke up.

I woke up to the sound of banging on my front door. It was about 3:00 a.m. When I got to the door, two police officers were standing there. I didn't understand. I was hours away from going to court to plead my case. I opened the door, and the officers began to read me my rights as they arrested me. I was shocked, and I didn't understand why. It felt like the floor dropped out from under me.

Two of my worst fears were coming to pass at the same time—losing my family and being locked up.

THE NEWS

It was a few months prior while I was at work when I got the news. I was working in a warehouse where we did electronic repair for Amazon. That's when I got the text from my mother-in-law: "She's with your brother, Eman." It was like a hole opened up inside of me. I ran to the bathroom. Reality seemed to change all around me. I couldn't believe it. How could my wife be with my brother? I could not believe this. I made myself not believe it. My wife and I were going through some difficulties, but how could this be happening?

Right then, a dream I had over a year before this flashed in my mind, "In the dream, I saw my wife on her knees in front of my brother kissing his feet." I remembered waking up from that dream upset and disturbed. I'd never had a thought like that enter my mind. I couldn't accept this as truth, so I had pushed it out of my mind.

I left work that day numb and hollow. I had lived alone in the condo since the separation except for when my daughter was with me. One night, I overheard my wife on the phone with my brother, telling him she loved him. She didn't know I heard this conversation. It became real. I couldn't deny it anymore. I called my brother and told him what I overheard, but he denied everything. I was so hurt, betrayed, angry, and overwhelmed with every emotion that leads to destruction. I decided to go downtown in my hurt to get drunk and pick up a girl.

My mind was made up, and I knew the exact drink I wanted to order to numb the pain. I was no drinker nor was I a cheater, but it seemed like the only thing I could do to have any sense of control in my bleeding sorrow. "Sometimes people will build their own floors instead of standing on the foundation that God has already built."

I went up to the bar to order my mojito, but what came out of my mouth was something that I'll never forget. The bartender looked at me and said, "What will it be?"

I answered back with confidence, "Ginger ale." Ginger ale? It was like something took over my words. What is happening?

The bartender looked at me with a confused and annoyed look. Then I knew God had just hijacked my carousing. I walked outside to a table by myself and sat there with my ginger ale. I began to get angry at God for what He did. I said aloud, "Fine! You won't let me drink, then I'm going to go down the street to the club and pick up a girl!" And I did go down to the club right then. I saw two beautiful ladies walking to the club, so I walked up to them and began to charm them the best I could. I walked in the club with them, and we sat at a table together.

As I looked at the girl in front of me, something happened that I had never experienced before. It was like a screen dropped down in front of me, and I saw this girl's life on the screen—details about what had happened to her when she was a teenager from her uncle and how he treated her this way, the things he said to her when she was little. It went on and on. I didn't know what to do, so I just began to tell this girl what I was seeing. Her eyes got real big and filled with water. She jumped up and ran to the bathroom. I had no idea what was happening.

Her friend looked at me and said, "Thank you, I'm a new Christian, and I've been trying to tell her about God. Everything you just said to her is all true." Then I looked at her, and the same thing happened. I told her what I saw, and then she ran to the bathroom. Now I was alone in the club, utterly confused about what was happening, but I knew it was God.

Eventually the ladies came back to the table in tears. I looked at them and said, "Uh, well I guess we should pray." So we all held hands and prayed. They thanked me, hugged me, and left. I sat there dumbfounded about what had just taken place. All my plans of destruction had failed because my God saw me in my dysfunction to show me mercy by awakening my spiritual gifts in my weakest time before I even knew Him. He showed me who I really was, although I didn't know yet.

The days that followed were empty and agonizing. The days seemed endless. Many nights I cried myself to sleep after putting my daughter to bed. Then one day, I received a call from my wife asking me to be ready to keep our daughter for a while. I asked her how long, but she said she didn't know. I asked her where she was going, but she would not tell me. We were not living together at that time. She disappeared, as far as I knew, and didn't tell anyone where she was going. I put out a missing person's report on her.

A month later, I received a text from my daughter's sitter telling me my wife and brother had come by and took my daughter with them. Another arrow came flying into my heart and soul. I called the police to remove the missing person's. I asked the officer if I could go there and get my daughter. He told me he could not tell me what to do but did not advise it. I asked God to show me the hotel they were staying in. In a city of more than six hundred thousand people, the Lord led me to a certain hotel. I did not see my brother's car, but I waited in the parking lot, anyway.

After a few hours, much to my surprise, my brother's car came pulling into the hotel lot. I prepared to confront them and bring my daughter back to her house. I prayed a simple prayer, "Lord, don't let me do anything stupid." I saw my wife, my brother, my daughter, and my brother's son get out of the car and walk across the parking lot. It seemed like it couldn't be reality but it was, so I made myself known. I looked at my brother and said, "What are you doing? This is my family. What are you doing?" My voice was calm and my words short. I spit at my brother but did not lay a finger on him. I picked up my daughter and turned to take her home. I knew the Lord had answered my prayer as I walked back to my car.

My wife followed behind, screaming at me. She did her best to stop me from putting our daughter in the car and keep me from driving away. Before I could drive away, my car was surrounded by people from inside the hotel. They were threatening my life as they cursed me. It was as though demons surrounded me. I slowly pulled forward and left.

A few weeks later, I was walking back from the store across a large field. Suddenly, just like before at the club, I saw a picture before my eyes. It was my wife downtown filing papers at the courthouse. I saw it very clearly. So I texted her and asked her, "Are you filing papers downtown?"

She called me. "Who told you that?"

I said, "No one told me that."

She told me it would be in my best interest to bring our daughter to her. I denied her request. The thought of my brother playing family with my wife and daughter made me deeply hurt and physically sick at the same time.

On one particular night, there was a knock at my door. It was late. I could see it was police officers so I opened the door. They identified me and read a no contact order filed against me from my wife. As they were reading the letter, the officers heard on the radio a call about one of their officer friends getting knifed and injured while he was pursuing a suspect. They did not want to be at my house, and I could feel their concern for their comrade. I asked them if I could pray for their friend. They prayed with me. Then they told me they had to remove my daughter from my house per the filed document. My daughter's mom was waiting outside to get her. The officer went upstairs with me and said, "This looks like a nice home. I hate to remove her from here, but we have to follow the court order." It felt like I was losing everything. They took my daughter and escorted her to her mom. The officer handed me the papers. I had two weeks until I had to go to family court.

HUMBLED PIE

One of the inmates I noticed was very quiet and kept to himself. I don't know why, but I was drawn to him. I approached him while he was sitting by himself at a table. He was very relaxed and did not seem like the other inmates. His face was without concern. I told him my situation. He calmly looked at me and said, "You will be fine." I asked why he was here. He said, "I'm just passing through."

I was facing a felony charge of wanton endangerment, a first-degree felony, and fourth-degree assault minor injury. She filed charges against me saying I had punched her to the ground, taken our daughter, and then tried to run her over with the car. Bond was set at twenty-five thousand dollars. I could feel the despair and hopelessness in the cell billow up like smoke rising into my lungs. I had never assaulted anyone in my adult life. I thought to myself, *How could she say these things about me? How could she have me locked up knowing the truth?*

Depression was like wet paint on everything in the place. Something in me knew I needed God's Word, so I desperately asked one of the guards for a Bible. Hours went by, but he brought me one. I opened it, and life began to touch me again. That place is so dark, it makes it evident what is good and what is evil. Sometimes in life, on the outside we can get complacent with God's truth. The ease and comfort of life can be very dangerous and actually lull us to sleep with compromise. So in some ways, spiritually speaking, jail was a part of God's mercy, and I was about to find out just how much.

He was persistent and would not stop asking me, "Just tear off one page in the back. Come on, man" over and over again. I finally gave in and he tore some pages out of the back of my little bible so he could roll his cigarette. My heart hurt afterwards.

We had no sense of time in there and the atmosphere made you feel like you would never get out and that the system doesn't even know who you are. The jail was overcrowded. After two days of sleeping on the cold concrete floor with no cot, they finally called my name. It felt like a gift wrapped in fear to be called by the guards. They moved me upstairs to a dorm-type cell. Filling in the hallway with the other names called, they had us all remove our clothes and searched us one by one with our hands up against the wall. It was humiliating—being treated like cattle, less than an animal. I was only a number and new offender in the eyes of the guard. But as we moved up and into my cell block, one of the guards looked at me and said, "What are you doing here?" It was like he could see the "not guilty" on me. I thought to myself, *He knows I'm not guilty. At least someone can see it.*

As I walked past the window pane of the dorm, it looked like chaos. As they opened the door, it sounded even worse. The volume was deafening, and everyone was talking at the same time. Everyone talked over one another as if the loudest was the strongest. Yells and outbursts erupted and rang out, reverberating off of the concrete walls. Thirty hardened criminals were locked up in one square box.

Two restless nights with hardly any sleep—the line between light and darkness was very tangible in that place. When the lights went out, they did not sleep. They got louder and more wild. It was like every demon in there began to manifest at night. There was no sleeping for anyone during the night, but when the noise finally died down, almost every night you could hear grown men in their beds sniffling. The quiet of the night exposes their hearts. It reminds them of where they are and what they've done.

One night as I lay on my cot, I was continually assaulted in my mind with the thoughts of my brother and wife together with my three-year-old daughter. And here I was lying in jail, falsely accused! It was complete despair. The demons were manifesting all around me in the cell. I was overwhelmed. I couldn't even think straight, so I lifted the covers over my head and cried out to God for the first time since being arrested. With tears running down my face, I cried out in a whisper with all of my heart, "Help me, God! I don't belong here. I'm innocent."

Immediately, I heard a voice speak to me.

"Eman, you're no more innocent than anyone in here."

I was stunned! The sound of His voice rang through every part of me. I knew it was the Lord Jesus, but I would have never expected to hear those words. I was expecting an angel or something to come and pat me on the back to tell me everything would be okay, but that is not what happened. One thing we must know about the Lord is that He will never tell you what you *want* to hear but always tell you the truth that you *need* to hear. Instantly, I understood what He meant. I thought I was innocent because I had been falsely accused and betrayed by my own family. The reality was that I was just as guilty as anyone in that jail. For we have all fallen short of the glory of God. I thought I was better than those inmates in that jail. I wasn't. I was the same—in desperate need of a savior. In the eyes of God, I was guilty of every sin.

My eyes had been opened, and I could see my self-righteousness. I could see everyone in my cell clearly without comparing myself to them. That's what most people do. They count the sins of others against them, and even if they never say anything, they think to themselves, *I would never do something like that.* They keep records of wrongs against people, especially people who have been incarcerated.

I knew God was using this opportunity to humble me. You can humble yourself before God or God can humble you *for you.* It's better that we humble ourselves, even in my natural situation, which by the world's standards was a great injustice. Be that as it may to God the rain falls on the just and the unjust alike. He is no respecter of persons. Yet He is a merciful God, and I was about to find out just how merciful He could be.

After fourteen days over the Thanksgiving holiday, my court date finally came. I had been fasting for four days, honestly trying to make God show me mercy, and He did but in His way. I was asleep the morning they called out my last name at two thirty in the morning, but my heart was wide awake. It was time for me to go before the judge. They lined us up in the hallway and had us lean against the wall and searched us. Then they put shackles on our feet and hands. I could feel the cold, sharp steel rubbing against my skin and bones. Then with a long chain, they chained us together at the waist and hands in a line. They led us through a maze of turns, and we kept going down what seemed like a basement of holding cells. I could feel the fear and anxiety in everyone. Most were terrified of their sentencing and what the judge would say to them. Literally, our future was just hours away in the hands of another.

There was no sense of time in the maze and no clocks anywhere to be found. I was disoriented and weak from fasting. They would take us to one holding cell then lock us in. Then to another, then another, like cattle going to the slaughter. Finally, we ended up in one big cell together with everyone who was going to court that morning. There was no sense of time, and we sat in the big room for a very long time. There were over fifty men in the big holding room. I had my Bible out as I sat against the wall. I was talking to the man next to me about God and life, and he was telling me about some things he had learned when suddenly both my ears became burning hot, and the sound of the chatter in the room became dull and muffled. Even the guy's voice who I was talking to became muffled, and I could no longer understand what he was saying. It was as if someone took their hands and placed them over my ears, but I could not see anyone doing it. No one in there was touching me, but someone was covering my ears and blocking out all of the sound in the room. I could feel the reality shift, and I was in shock.

That's when I heard a voice speak to me and say, *"Eman, I want you to stand up and pray for everyone in here!"*

I was shaken by the sound of this voice. It was like before but much stronger. All my senses and awareness of my outward condition was gone. The words of the voice still ringing in my ears and through every molecule of my being. A sudden fear came over me that I had never known. It was as if I did not do what this voice told me to do then I would die right on the spot! I was shaken to the core. I did not know what was happening, but one thing I did know was that I had to obey this voice. I sat my Bible down, still in shock, and stood up. I addressed the room of cold-blooded murders, rapists, robbers, thieves, and thugs.

"We are all here going to court before a judge, right?" I cried out, then I was interrupted by two famous bank-robbing brothers. Hate and mocking laughter spewed out at me, and I could see the demons come through them at me from across the room.

Then a man leaning against the far wall yelled out to me, "Go ahead, man!"

Suddenly a boldness came over me and I spoke, "We are all going before a judge today, but there is a judge higher than the judge that we will all face today. He is the one who gave authority to the judges because He is the one who has all the authority. So I call on Him to be your judge today. God, I thank you for these men, and I bless them and the judges you have given authority to. In Jesus name, Amen."

Then as soon as I said, "amen," the door unlocked and swung open. A guard began to call inmates names in groups of five or six. I was called into a group of five other inmates. We were escorted, chained together, up three flights of stairs and into a cramped holding cell beside the courtroom.

The room was a tiny, concrete cell and had one metal bed across the back wall and one metal toilet in the corner. The door was metal with a small, glass window down the center. No one was talking much. I could sense the nerves in the room—fear even. Then something happened that I could not explain. It was like one of those moments in time where you say something and the words that come out of your mouth don't match up with your brain and you immediately regret speaking them. I looked at the group and said, "What if I told you that everyone in this room was going to be OR today?" If you're unfamiliar, being OR means the court releases an inmate on their Own Recognizance. It's for first-time offenders.

After I said that, they all looked at me very intensely. Then they began to look at one another and began shaking their heads in agreement. Now I didn't know what to do. I knew it was God that spoke through me, but these men were not first time offenders. They were hardened criminals who had probably not heard the words "OR" in many years. I was in way over my head with this. I didn't know what to do, but they were in agreement, so I said, "Okay, well I guess we should pray." I had everyone hold hands in a circle because everyone knows circles are holy. The truth is, I was making this up as I went along, not knowing what I was doing and had never done anything like this before. I began to pray for the judge and the prosecuting attorney and bless them with the love of God.

At the end of the prayer everyone said, "Amen." I could sense a change in the room. It was like the air was energized, which now I recognize as faith.

After a little while, the first inmate was called into court. We all waited silently for him to return. He came back and said, "They OR'd me!" He said he has never seen that judge so happy before. She is usually very hard on everyone, but today she was happy. We all could feel excitement, but we didn't get our hopes up because it was only one of the six of us, so we kept silent about it.

A few minutes later, the next inmate was called. He came back sooner than the first, saying with excitement, "They OR'd me!" The little room began to buzz, but a very hushed expectation began to rise. The next two inmates who went to court and came back with the same verdict!

Now, the next inmate was a man with such a long record, it dated back to his high school years. He knew the judge and prosecuting attorney by first name—not in a good way. His most recent charge was fourteen counts of armed robbery with a deadly weapon, easily ten to fifteen years with his record. They called his name, and he went before the judge. Twenty minutes later, he returned and said, "They OR'd me!"

We were all in amazement, recognizing the hand of God in our midst. They were all so excited, and I didn't know what to do. All these men, except one, would be released today as free men. I said to them, "Okay now you have to be good and not do bad things and go to church." I honestly didn't know what to say to them. It was a true miracle.

Now it was my turn to face this judge who had let these criminals go home. My attorney spoke to me in the hallway. "The judge knows your wife is lying, the prosecuting attorney knows she is lying, and when we get the video footage from outside the hotel, she will have felony charges filed against her from the state for filing a false report which is a felony charge. The court dropped the felony charge against you, but they want you to plead guilty for the misdemeanor of fourth degree assault but we are not going to do that."

Right then, I heard a voice speak to me and saw an image of a cross in my imagination. *"Eman, I plead guilty for something I didn't do for you. Will you do the same for her?"*

The voice was so loud in my being it took a minute to hear what my attorney was saying to me. His voice reverberated off of the walls of my mind. I knew that voice now was the voice of Jesus, the only true God. He had been guiding me and leading me this whole time, speaking to me and teaching me. I told my attorney I was going to plead guilty for the misdemeanor. He was baffled and did not understand why I would do that, knowing that I was innocent. But the Lord had taught me a valuable lesson in my most vulnerable state. "I'm no more innocent than anyone in that jail." And even though what she did was wrong, we all make mistakes, and Jesus paid a price for all of us. If He has shown us mercy and died for us while we were yet sinners, how can we not show that same mercy to those who have sinned against us?

I knew what I had to do. I turned to my attorney and said, "I'm pleading guilty to the assault charge." He looked at me like I was crazy knowing that I was innocent. He tried his best to get me to change my mind. There was no changing my mind. The fear of the Lord was on me, and I was hearing the voice of God speaking to me. I could not go back now. I stepped towards the judge and pleaded guilty. I was released that same day.

As I left my jail cell, many inmates came up to me and hugged me and thanked me for helping them. They honored me by calling me "preacher man." It was very humbling.

The next day, I was at my condo trying to adjust to my whole world being turned upside down—the loss of all my jobs, my wife living with my brother and divorcing me, and my daughter caught in the middle of it all. My phone rang, and it was my brother who wanted to meet with me. He came over but stayed outside in his car. I remember walking up to his car, and I had some things that I wanted to say to him that were not Christ-like. He rolled down his window and began to threaten me out of fear for the courts and his own son.

I looked at him, and this is what came out of my mouth: "I love you and forgive you, and I bless you and pray that every plan and purpose that God has for your life will come to pass in Jesus' name." I was shocked that it happened again! Words coming out of my mouth that I didn't ask for or think about beforehand.

He looked away from me and threatened me again and cursed me. I looked at him and said again, "I love you and forgive you and bless you that every plan and purpose that God has for your life will come to pass in Jesus's name."

He cursed me again. Again I said, "I love you and forgive you, and I bless you that every plan and purpose that God has for you will come to pass in Jesus's name."

Again he cursed me, and a fourth time I said the same. Then he threatened my life. As I walked back to my home, my mind was swarming. How could those words have come out of my mouth? I didn't feel like I forgave him. The reality was I felt the opposite feelings of forgiveness or love. All these thoughts raced through my mind, then all of a sudden I heard two voices speak to me as I entered my house.

The first voice said, *"You don't really forgive him because you don't feel like you do."* This voice was correct that I didn't feel like I forgave him, but then another voice spoke to me, and I knew it was the Lord Jesus who said, *"Eman, remember what I said in my Word. What comes out of a man's mouth comes out of his heart. You speak forgiveness. How you feel does not dictate the true position of your heart. What you speak shows you the true position of your heart. You spoke forgiveness so this is the true position of your heart. All you have to do is use faith and believe you forgive and eventually your emotions will line up with the truth."*

I was in total shock. I had never heard anything like this in my life. It turned out to be one of the single most important moments in my life. So I obeyed the Lord and used faith to believe I forgave anytime the enemy tried to poke at my emotions. Exactly what Jesus said came to pass just as He said it would. I don't even remember the moment it happened, but the feelings and emotions of hurt and pain were completely wiped out of my heart and life and even more than that, a great love began to fill me toward my brother and even for my ex-wife.

We must love one another as we love ourselves. We must love ourselves because the truth is that if God loves you, you are worth loving, and if God Has forgiven you in Christ, then you are worth forgiving. Release that same forgiveness to everyone else who has wronged you or caused you pain by sinning against you. Do this by His Spirit living within you. Hold no record of wrongs against anyone. This is true freedom in Christ Jesus.

God wants us free from ourselves and free from others—not free from others to not care for them but so free from them that we are able to love them how God loves them, unconditionally. People treat people a certain way according to the outcome they think they are going to get. This is a mindset of conditional love. But how we treat people should be a manifestation of the love of God for who He has made them to be, not how they are treating us. If we only treat people according to how they are treating us, then we are not being sons and daughters of God. If the Lord has treated us as sons and died for us while we were still in our sins, how can we still treat one another as enemies when God has treated us as beloved?

I believe the Lord wants us to forgive and release people out of our hearts so He can give us a new heart and fill it with the fullness of heaven in Christ. It's not prayer that you need to be able to do this. Use your faith right now and speak forgiveness out loud and release whoever you need to and bless them. You can say it like this:

"I forgive _____ and I release them out of my heart in the name of Jesus. I hold nothing against _____ any longer and I command all bitterness to leave me in Jesus' name. I bless _____ in the name of Jesus."

No matter how you feel or what your emotions are saying, speak this out loud. It is very important. God didn't "think" the world into existence. He spoke, and it came into being! It takes faith to forgive, and we all have a portion of faith that God has given us. Use it by speaking forgiveness in this simple way and believe that what you have spoken is what's really in your heart—not what you are feeling. Any time the enemy tries to come and make you feel those familiar feelings, simply thank God that you did forgive and say, "I bless _____ in Jesus' name." It might happen immediately or it may take time but eventually your emotions will line up with the truth of forgiveness.

CHAPTER 7

TESTING, TRIALS, AND FIRE

Most people spend their lives trying to avoid trials. Most naturally don't like change or hardships. We spend a lot of effort living in ways that tend to keep us "safe" and "comfortable." The animal kingdom does this. It is survival of the fittest, living life for the benefit of oneself, for family, and maybe even for friends. It is always living in fear of the "what if." It is living in a way that avoids uncomfortable experiences that will keep you from really experiencing the goodness and full salvation of the Lord in this life.

Since the fall of man in the garden of Eden, man has tried desperately to make life easier by continually trying to attain the ease we once lived in in the garden, the way God originally designed it. The problem is that there is a real enemy, named Satan, who comes to steal, kill, and destroy. He was given power to rule this world. Let's be clear. Jesus has defeated Satan and has taken back the keys to death and the grave, destroying the power of sin on the cross (see Hebrews 2:14–15). Yet Satan is still here, roaming around *like a roaring lion,* seeking whom he may devour.

"Be sober-minded; be watchful. Your adversary the devil prowls around like a roaring lion, seeking someone to devour" (1 Peter 5:8).

The devil is doing this from a position of defeat even though he is the prince of the power of the air because he is already defeated. Only God knows all the reasons He has allowed it to be this way. One reason is so that we, the children of light, might receive the honor to partake in destroying the works of Satan, expanding the kingdom of God on earth as it is in heaven and bringing glory to God until the return of our King, Jesus!

Jesus promises us that we will encounter trials in this life and gives comfort and instruction on how to respond to such trials.

"I have told you all this so that you may have peace in me. Here on earth you will have many trials and sorrows. But take heart, because I have overcome the world" (John 16:33).

He who is in us, Jesus the Mighty One, the Righteous One, the Lord of Glory, the Prince of Peace, the Wonderful Counselor, Mighty God, Everlasting Father (see Isaiah 9:6)—He has overcome the world and is alive in us! We should have great joy and thanksgiving should be within us. This is how we shine in a dark world and shine like the stars (see 1 Thessalonians 5:16–18).

"And if children, then heirs-heirs of god and fellow heirs with Christ, provided we suffer with him in order that we may also be glorified with him" (Romans 8:17).

We are called to be "Christ-like." We are called to be like Jesus. As the scripture tells us, in order to *truly* be an heir with Christ, we must suffer with Him. When the appointed time came, Jesus drank the cup of suffering and passed that chalice to us for the honor of partaking in His glory with Him. Many run from this offering from God, revealing that they have not truly denied all of "themselves" and picked up their cross to follow Him.

> *Then Jesus told his disciples, "If anyone would come after me, let him deny himself and take up his cross and follow me. For whoever would save his life will lose it, but whoever loses his life for my sake will find it." (Matthew 16:24–25)*

The Lord revealed to me that when He spoke of taking up the cross that it is an act of embrace. The cross is a sign of forgiveness of sins but also of suffering. When we deny ourselves and pick up our cross, what we are actually doing is giving up our lives and embracing suffering with Christ. Most believers that I meet do not understand or have revelation of picking up their cross. As a result, they spend a lot of time trying to avoid suffering and running from the enemy instead of conquering over the enemy with Christ, which is a part of our inheritance. You see, Christ defeated Satan by going to the cross (embracing the cup of suffering).

The word is clear that we are not to be afraid of the enemy. We have not been given the spirit of fear, but the spirit of love, power, and a sound mind. If we keep our minds on Christ, He will keep our hearts in perfect peace. As it says in Isaiah,

> *You will guard him and keep him in perfect and constant peace whose mind [both its inclination and its character] is stayed on You, because he commits himself to You, leans on You and hopes confidently in You. (Isaiah 26:3 AMP)*

Let's commit ourselves to Jesus completely. The alternative is to live a selfish, self-focused life in fear and being intimidated by the enemy which tosses us back and forth, living in misery and dread instead of ruling and reigning with Christ.

The reality is that we need trials, fire, and testing. It's the only way to reveal and prove our faith in Christ. In Romans 5, there is a sequence of suffering that is outlined. It explains what kind of fruit is produced by suffering when we go through it.

> *Therefore, since we have been justified by faith, we have peace with God through our Lord Jesus Christ. Through Him we have also obtained access by faith into this grace in which we stand, and we rejoice in hope of that glory of God. Not only that, but we rejoice in our sufferings, knowing that suffering produces endurance, and endurance produces character, and character produces hope, and hope does not put us to shame, because God's love has been poured into our hearts through the Holy Spirit who has been given to us. (Romans 5:1–5)*

Let's do what Jesus tells us to do—rejoice and embrace suffering. We stand at the edge of victory and the washing water of the Word of Christ cleanses us with faith in Him. We should step into it and be unafraid to run this race and run as hard as we can by the power of the Holy Spirit!

APPROACHING TRIALS OF TESTING

We need to understand what the Word of God says about trials and the reason why they are promised to come. We discussed the suffering and how the Lord allows this to produce character within us. In scripture, we find a key reasoning behind the fiery trials.

> *Beloved, do not be surprised at the fiery trial when it comes upon you to test you, as though something strange were happening to you. But rejoice insofar as you share Christ's sufferings, that you may also rejoice and be glad when his glory is revealed. If you are insulted for the name of Christ, you are blessed, because the Spirit of glory and of God rests upon you. (1 Peter 4:12–14 AMPC)*

The Spirit of glory and of God is resting upon you. This is an amazing reality! Oftentimes people get so offended and hurt when they are insulted for the name of Christ. They step back and turn down the fire of God on the inside of them. They question themselves and God. This is a trick of the enemy. He wants you to focus on yourself and to question in your heart God's will for your life. Don't fall for this. Know who you are in Christ and that you belong to the Father, His glory is upon you, and you are a shining light that is exposing darkness everywhere you go. You are lighting the way for others to follow and to know Christ!

> *In this you rejoice, though now for a little while, if necessary, you have been grieved by various*

trials, so that the tested genuineness of your faith more precious than gold that perished though it is tested by fire may be found to result in praise and glory and honor at the revelation of Jesus Christ. (1 Peter 1:6–7)

REJOICING IN TRIALS

The best thing we can do when we see a trial ahead of us is to run towards it as hard as we can with all the energy that Jesus works so mightily in us (see Samuel 17:48–51). We must run forward with all confidence and with all our love in God. Like little David, the shepherd boy running at Goliath the giant who was cursing the living God, David had no war training in the typical sense. He was just a kid who knew how to love and worship God. He knew how to spend time with God in the secret place. He developed a real relationship with Him, a romance of song and worship where the love of God became his reality, living and dwelling in the presence of the Lord.

David took no thought for his own life. He didn't even consider the possibility that he could lose the fight. All he knew was the mouth of the enemy had to be shut and his head removed. He knew killing Goliath was the right thing to do. He knew the forces of the enemy who profaned God must be scattered. He burned with a consuming fire against the evil insolence of the enemy toward the people of the Living God. This is how we must confront the evil that encamps around us. This is how we must act when faced with opposition from the enemy. God is seeking people who know how to worship Him in spirit and in truth. Our worship and love of Jesus and His love for us qualifies us to run with a fire from the throne of God toward the enemy, fearlessly challenging him with exactly what God is going to do.

We must become a fearless people in the face of trials and fire. We must put on the love of Christ and stop tiptoeing around the enemy, hoping he won't hear us going by. We must stop trying to get by the enemy, and we must put up our shield of faith and pull out our sword of the spirit, which is the truth of Jesus and the blood covenant. There is no devil that can stand against the blood of Jesus. We must believe that we are painted in the blood of Jesus. We have become engrafted in the royal family of God with the implanted Word in us, making us a living, breathing, and walking sword of God. Empowered by the Holy Ghost by our faith in Jesus Christ, we are God's weapon of choice to destroy the works of the enemy. We partner with God to set people free by the truth of the crucifixion and resurrection of Christ Jesus, our Lord.

Shadrach, Meshack, and Abednego were three men who refused to submit to the fear of a king who wanted to make himself a god. They refused to worship another god. With only integrity and no Holy Ghost, they took no thought for their lives, they stood and refused to bow to the enemy. The love of God consumed them and fear had no place in them. The power and mercy of God stood with them, making the flames of the enemy obsolete. The Lord, who is the eternal fire of God, delivered them from the hand of the enemy. In the same way, we can stand in love and confidence in Jesus, our Deliverer. He will stand with us in the fiery trials that the enemy has set for us. We will not be afraid. God will strengthen us as we set out soul in stillness and know that our Father is God. By faith, we will enter into the rest of God. Our eyes will stay on Jesus and our bodies will be full of light (see Matthew 6:22). We will look to Jesus and become radiant with joy and our faces will never be ashamed (see Psalms 34:5). God will cover us with His feathers and comfort us under His wings (see Psalms 91). One walking in faith is dominant, and no forces of darkness will be able to stand. So we take dominion over fear and trepidation, and it is crushed under the hooves of the war horses of praise. The angel armies of the Lord are with us with the might of the fiery chariots of God. We are the sons of God. We are royal priests of a Holy nation. Our sufferings in Christ have made us heirs with Him in glory!

Trials will produce patience in the joy of the Lord. This causes us to gain endurance through perseverance, developing the character of the believer who is a light shining in the darkness. Our hope is in Jesus Christ because in His name alone is the hope of the world (see

Matthew 12:21). The glory that will be revealed in us makes the sufferings of the present time irrelevant because Jesus is Lord of all and has written our names in His Book of Life.

The integrity of our character is important when we go through trials and hardships. After we pass through it, we become qualified in that area by heaven, giving us confidence to practice our authority. You will realize how sweet and precious suffering and hardships are in your life—no longer fearing them but meeting them head on covered in the armor of God with banners of victory lifted high!

PRAYER

"Father God, help us Jesus. Give us Your heart to worship you with the purest of love. Establish in us a peace that laughs at the attacks of the enemy. Give us a passion and desire in our hearts to worship you in the secret place, contending to know you more, praising you with our whole heart. Jesus, we want to fall more in love with you. Replace our crying with confidence in you in all faith. You are all in all, Lord. Help us believe that we are free in you. Amen."

Jesus gives us three personal examples of how He responded to storms. In the first example, He was asleep in the middle of a storm. The peace that lived in Him was so great that the circumstances around Him could not disturb Him. What was in Him was greater than what was around Him. He was sleeping so well that the disciples thought they needed to wake Him up or they would all die because of the violence of the storm. He who lives in us is greater than he who lives in the world. Jesus displays rest at its best.

When the disciples woke Him up, He rebuked them for their unbelief but showed us another example. He demonstrated that storms can also be defeated by speaking to them. Sometimes you can't just sit back and do nothing, but you must speak to the mountain so it can move out of your way. Most people do not understand the power in what they speak. If they did, they would be more careful about what they said every day. When you speak, you are either speaking life or death, blessing or curse.

The last example of Jesus responding to storms is found in Matthew 14:22–33. This is when Jesus walked on water. He fully displays His authority over the storm as He decides to walk on the storm. This completely captivates Jesus's attitude and power over the elemental principles of this world. Jesus is showing us that He is Lord over this world and is asking us to follow Him.

PRAYER

"Lord, give us the trust to rest in the most troubled waters and give us the boldness to speak to every wave of the enemy while you lead us in every step over the stormy depths in Jesus's name."

We must worship in the trials. Worship was what made David a man after God's own heart. It's what separated him from everyone else. His adoration for the Lord is shown all throughout the Psalms. Heaven is longing for the bride of Christ to join in on its song of praise. When will our worship line up with the purity of the worthiness of Jesus? All of our worship should lift His name up high and praise Him! He is worthy of all praise! When we worship like David did, Jesus should be our only focus. His presence should melt us, and His love should overwhelm us. We need to turn all of our affections and attention to Him. Our only motive must be because He is worthy.

> *For we do not have a high priest who cannot sympathize with our weaknesses, but one who has been tempted in all things as we are, yet without sin. Therefore let us draw near with confidence to the throne of grace, so that we may receive mercy and find grace to help in time of need. (Hebrews 4:15–16)*

Coming boldly to the throne of grace is not simply praying a louder prayer. I see many people who pray from a place of fear, worry, anxiety, doubt, and stress. None of these attributes belong to a child in the kingdom of God and are not attributes of our Heavenly Father, either. Believe that our high priest, Jesus Christ, has been tempted in all things as we are. We can have assurance that He sympathizes and understands our struggles and has conquered each and every one of them.

> *Behold and hour is coming, and has already come, for you to be scattered, each to his own home and to leave me alone; and yet I am not alone, because the Father is with me. These things I have spoken to you, so that in Me you may have peace. In the world you will have tribulation, but take courage (be of good cheer), I have overcome the world. (John 16:32–33)*

Jesus promises us that we will have trouble in this world. One of the biggest issues and lies of the evil one is that when we believe in Jesus, we will no longer have troubles, and if we *do* have troubles, then there must be something wrong with us. This lie instills doubt and fear in the body of Christ and a false sense of victory. He promises us troubles in this life and then declares for us to be of good cheer and even courageous in the face of tribulation because He has overcome the world. My question is, "How has He overcome the world if in this world we will still have trouble?" He is not called the Prince of Peace for nothing! Jesus is not a firefighter. He has all the power to put out your fires, and in some cases, He will. However, He prefers standing with you as you stand in faith surrendered to His goodness in the midst of the fire. Living in perfect peace, completely untouched or burned, not even smelling like smoke, totally unaffected by the works of the enemy to destroy the temple of God! This gives Him glory; this pleases Him (our faith in Him and faith that we are sons and daughters in His kingdom). Jesus gives us a picture of what it looks like as He has conquered the storms in this world and in yours.

Jesus slept in the middle of the storm until unbelief, fueled by fear in His disciples, woke Him. He spoke to the storm, and it calmed. In the next account, He walked on the storm. The Prince of Peace walking on the storm—this is our King! This is our Lord. This is our beautiful friend and conqueror. He has given us the same authority and power to either rest through our trials in His presence, speak to them with His authority He has given us, or to walk on them with our eyes fixed on Him. This should fill us with confidence in Him who lives in us. We can come into His throne room of grace with our requests, whatever they may be, in peace and confidence that our Father has the power to do it. His love for us is wrapped in His grace, power, and joy. We are secured in it by His victory through Jesus.

CHAPTER 8

LOVE AND HEALING

Often when the body of Christ prays in times of need, they lift up prayers that are not filled with faith but filled with other things. For instance, when a loved one has been hospitalized, "believers" will pray desperate prayers and become frustrated and hurt because their loved one is not healed. They, then, come up with all sorts of excuses as to why a prayer did not work or even be arrogant enough to try to explain why God did not heal someone. This mindset and attitude really reveals the reality of one's relationship with the Father. People get emotional when a loved one is sick or hospitalized and then they pray desperate prayers, putting emotions before faith. It's not wrong to be emotional. In fact, we read in the Gospels how emotional Jesus got at the tomb of Lazarus. He wept. The difference Jesus displays in the story of Lazarus is in how He responded when He received the news of the illness.

> Now a certain man was ill, Lazarus of Bethany, the village of Mary and her sister Martha. It was Mary who anointed the Lord with ointment and wiped His feet with her hair, whose brother Lazarus was ill. So the sisters went to Him, saying, "Lord, he whom you love is ill." But when Jesus heard it He said, "This illness does not lead to death, It is for the

glory of God, so that the Son of God may be glorified through it." (John 11)

Jesus's response to the bad news is faith! He spoke life in the face of death. Before He ever got to the tomb, He was operating from heaven to earth. The language of heaven is faith. Jesus was not overwhelmed with fear or worry. He believed God. In the next passage, He actually demonstrates the first action of His faith motivated by love. Verse 5 reads, "Now Jesus loved Martha and her sister and Lazarus. So, when He heard that Lazarus was ill, he stayed two days longer in the place where He was. Then after this, He said to the disciples, 'Let us go to Judea again.'" This amazing strength is on display in the faith of Jesus. Jesus didn't run to the tomb as soon as He got the news. He spoke life and words of faith then demonstrated His faith by staying two more days. Jesus loved them so He stayed away longer. This does not make logical sense, but it's reassuring that God is not logical according to our own standards! Jesus wanted them to believe in the Son of God and for God to be glorified. This was better than Him rushing to Lazarus to heal him before he died.

God always compels us into the faith that we need to step into His reality. When we allow Him to stretch our faith, we go up to the next level of glory. Our reality apart from His reality is a false reality.

They all had faith that Jesus could heal the illness, but they did not yet have the faith needed for the resurrection power of the dead. God was calling them into this kind of faith. He was calling them higher because Jesus's death was coming soon.

Jesus said, "These signs shall follow those that believe," meaning healings and miracles. So the disconnect is not on God's end. Believers often confuse emotional desire for their loved one to be healed with faith working through love. Jesus demonstrated faith working through love with Lazarus before He demonstrated emotions by weeping with everyone. He has given us everything we need to rule and reign in this life and the one to come. The prayer of faith is not something we can do on our own. We have a helper, the mighty Holy Spirit, and He wants us to walk with Him, to commune with Him, and to listen to Him when He speaks to us. It is always beneficial to obey the Holy Spirit. God will not lead you into destruction. He will not guide you into despair. You can trust in your heavenly Father. Jesus will never leave you nor forsake you. He loves you. We need to step higher to the next faith and bring glory to the Father. We need to stop focusing on ourselves and start loving the one in front of us.

I remember one morning in particular when God wanted to bring glory to His Son, Jesus. It was February 14, 2014. I woke up early and got ready for work four hours early. The joy of the Lord was on me in a way that was noticeable to me. I had energy that I knew was from the Holy Spirit. Without hesitation, as soon as I was dressed for work, I put my daughter in the van and left to find a babysitter for my work day. It came to my mind to ask my aunt who lived at a retirement home. I parked out front of the building and called her. She agreed to watch my daughter for me, but I had to wait an hour.

As I sat there waiting, I saw a school bus stop just ahead of me in front of a gas station. A young girl got off the bus carrying a pink cake box. I watched her walk from the bus over to the gas station. I thought to myself, *Why am I watching this girl carry this cake box?* Right then, I heard the Holy Spirit say, "*Go!*" I knew He wanted me to go pray for that girl.

I drove over and pulled up to the gas station. I stepped out of the van as the girl was standing outside the store. That's when I saw the boot on her foot. I thought to myself, *Of course God wants me to pray for her foot.* I asked her if I could pray for her foot, and she gave me a very awkward "Sure." So I prayed for her foot to be healed. Nothing happened except she felt awkward, and I felt her awkwardness. She thanked me and left. I thought, *Well that was very uneventful.*

Right then, a woman burst out of the gas station and yelled out, "We are closed! No one can come in or out for the next ten minutes. The ambulance and police are on their way!"

She seemed terrified, so I walked over to her and asked, "Are you okay?"

She said again in fear, "No one in or out for the next ten minutes! The ambulance and police are on their way. A girl just died here." Right then something came over me, and with a big smile, I looked at her and said, "Well then you need to let me come inside and pray for her."

She looked at me and replied, "Okay. You can come in but nobody else."

I walked into the gas station and looked down one of the aisles and saw a young woman lying flat on her back. She was purple in her face, which I could see as I got closer. There was an older lady and a young man who were at her feet, fearfully panicking. I know they meant well, but fear and panic has never glorified God. I asked them to move aside so I could pray for her. She had no pulse and was not breathing. Her face was blue, and no color was left in her skin. I reached down and placed my hand under her head and my other hand on her forehead. She was cold to the touch. I began to pray for her and command life to come and death to leave in Jesus's name.

About five minutes passed, and the older lady and young man began to interrupt again. I could tell it was the enemy trying to stop what God was wanting to do because of the way that it annoyed me. Even though they meant well, they were operating out of fear. It's one of the reasons Jesus put people out of the room when He raised the young girl from the dead. I looked at them and said, "No! Can't you see I'm praying for her?"

They fell silent. I turned back and continued to pray, moving to the other side of her body. I could tell there were many people surrounding us, but I was locked onto this young woman and didn't look. After about fifteen minutes of commanding life and the spirit of death to leave, I saw with my own eyes pink color return to her lifeless face. Then her mouth opened, and she gasped for air! Her eyes opened then rolled back in her head. She began to make so many sounds out of her mouth—sounds I had never heard a human make before. I couldn't tell if the Holy Spirit was going in or demons were coming out. With one final scream, her eyes rolled forward, and she looked at me.

I sat her up and said, "Jesus has healed you. Do you understand?"

She nodded her head "yes," then I looked behind me, and all the EMS workers and policemen were standing behind me with their mouths open, just watching and not saying a word. I lifted the girl up onto her feet and gave her a hug and blessed her.

One of the ambulance guys said with fear in his voice, "Well... We need to take her into the unit and check her out."

I told her to go with them and that she would be fine. I stood outside as they checked her out in the unit. I stood with the police officers and told him they were going to be seeing God do more things like this. He said, "I hope so." They released the girl and said she was perfectly healed and all the tests read normal. I walked with the young lady and told her what Jesus did for her. She began to cry and told me that her grandfather was a pastor, but she had run from the church and from Jesus. I shared the gospel with her, and she gave her life back to Jesus, who had spared her life.

We serve a God who raises the dead. His power and might is greater than anyone or any devil. His love is mighty to save. He wants to bring us into His reality where we see His beauty and are captivated by His love.

After the girl was raised from the dead, I asked the Lord why the policemen or EMS workers didn't stop me when they arrived on the scene but just watched. I asked this because I know that when they arrive, then it becomes their jurisdiction. He spoke to me and said, "They had no authority when they arrived on the scene to take over jurisdiction because I was already on the scene. That's why they could not speak." The Lord is with us. He is mighty and wonderful. His presence will manifest around us. He is active, alive, and is doing many great and wonderful things all over the world. He wants us to join in on the fun! For that to happen, we must deny ourselves, pick up our cross *daily*, and follow Him. Being willing and available vessels for the Lord will sometimes interrupt our plans. It may make us get up four hours earlier than we need to or change plans that we have made because God wants us to be in a certain place at a certain time for a specific purpose that we might not even know about until we obey the leading of the Spirit in faith. Following Jesus is not convenient and will not fit nicely into your schedule for the week. We submit to God, not the other way around. Our hearts must be willing to yield to the voice of the Lord at any moment, understanding that our lives are not our own. We were bought at a price. Now, I'm not saying you have to do this. But if you want a life filled with the miraculous, with signs and wonders, the power of God being released, divine appointments, and the dead raising, then you will have to surrender to God's schedule. It will take faith and put other things in your life in the back seat to His will.

God's love is what changes the heart of men. I remember when the Holy Spirit interrupted one of my prayers one day to teach me this lesson. You may be thinking, *How rude of Him to interrupt me while I'm trying to serve him.* There are times when people would interrupt me, and I would get very annoyed. This was before the Lord regenerated my heart. Some people think that any interference to stop prayers must be from the enemy. I've found that in most cases this couldn't be further from the truth. When this interruption came, I was going out and praying for anyone I could see. Up to this point, I had been going out on my own for four months, praying for people and seeing more than half the people I prayed for healed. It was a very exciting time!

On the last day of a conference I was attending, I went out with a team to pray for people at a mall. I saw a man walking across the parking lot with a cane and limping severely. I stopped him and asked him what had happened. He told me that He had a bad hip and was going into surgery in the morning for a hip replacement. He had been off of work for a few months because of it. I asked him if I could pray for his hip. He said yes, so I knelt down and began praying. Suddenly, in the middle of my prayer, I hear the Holy Spirit say to me, "Eman, you're not loving him." I was shocked! Stunned even.

Holy Spirit had interrupted me but rightfully so. As it says in 1 Corinthians 14–29,

> *Two or three prophets should speak, and the others should weigh carefully what is said, and if a revelation comes to someone who is sitting down, the first speaker should stop.*

I was the first speaker, rattling off my formulated prayer for healing, which up until that point, I believed had been tried and tested as "just the right way to pray for healing." However, by me approaching this man in this way, the Holy Spirit had become the prophet who was sitting down, and that's never a good position to put Him in. I was not honoring His presence and power. I was trying to lead God. I was not operating in love which meant that my prayer had no power or authority. Rather, just religious repetition and nowhere near the fruits and law of love. The Holy Spirit had the revelation as the scripture says, because He *is* the revelation.

He interrupted me in the middle of my ninja healing prayer where nothing was happening in the natural, anyway. He said, "Eman, you're not loving him." Wow! I was completely blindsided. I thought, *Here I am kneeling down in the middle of a busy mall parking lot to pray for this man's hip. How could I not be loving him? Can't you see what I am doing?* Talk about risk. I was exposed in the open.

I paused for a long time before I spoke again. I said, "Can I pray again?"

He said, "Okay..."

I waited. The Holy Spirit then began to show me how God sees him as a son in the kingdom, paid for with the highest price. Then compassion filled my spirit and the Holy Spirit fell on this man. He yelped, "Oh! Oh! Oh! It's on fire, it's on fire!"

I was just as shocked as he was. I said, "That's good! Check it out, man. Do what you couldn't do before!"

He kept bending over and over, squatting down over and over. He even did a few jumps. He was in complete amazement at this miracle. He was so happy and filled with energy and joy. He threw his cane over his shoulder and said, "I'm going to go back to work tomorrow!" He no longer needed surgery because Jesus had completely and totally healed him. He walked back to his car with his cane over his shoulder.

Father God was trying to teach me something very important. A question came into my heart. "What's more important? To heal someone or to love them?" To love is the ultimate goal of the Father's heart, nature, and expression. The best part about becoming His love is that healing comes with it. The Lord was teaching me we can go out and pray for everyone, but that doesn't mean we are loving them. One of the most arresting points God has shared with me about this reality is that people can be healed but still not changed.

I've seen people healed right before my eyes, yet at the same time, nothing changed in them! I remember asking, "God, how can someone experience healing yet still not be changed?" Every time I would ask this or ponder this question, the Lord responded in the same way, "Eman, change doesn't happen in the healing. It happens in the heart." Time after time, this rang true. I could see the difference in someone being just healed versus someone loved. The Father's love flowing through us is the ultimate goal. Healing is an attribute of who Jesus is in His compassion. His supernatural love is the only thing that will change the hearts of people. He showed me that He is encountering us all and that at different points in our lives, we experience Him. We all have encounters until we have the one encounter that makes us fall in love with Him, then everything changes. We must seek first His kingdom, who is Jesus—who is love.

PRAYER

"Lord, help us to seek love before miracles and help us to see people how you see them. Give us your heart for the lost and broken so we never walk by anyone who needs you and don't experience your compassion for them. In Jesus's name. Amen."

CHAPTER 9

THE LOVE OF JESUS

Sometimes when you are completely surrounded by an impossible situation that seems hopeless, and none of your efforts could possibly bring about change, right at that moment is when the Holy Spirit becomes the only possible solution. This is the place we should contend to stay in at all times. Cry out to God in the secret place for Him to keep you in the place of knowing that by your own power, nothing is accomplished and to rely on Him in all situations for all things. The name of Jesus is our hope (see Matthew 12:21).

> *Love is patient and kind, Love is not jealous or boastful or proud or rude. It does not demand its own way. It is not irritable, and it keeps no record of being wronged. It does not rejoice about injustice but rejoices whenever the truth wins out. Love never gives up, never loses faith, is always hopeful, and endures through every circumstance. Love never fails. (1 Corinthians 13:4–7 NLT)*

I saw the love of our Father once capture the heart and eyes of a homeless man. It was a late summer night. I was very tired and wanted to go to sleep, but I found myself driving downtown. I really didn't feel like praying or ministering to anyone. As soon as I parked, I saw a homeless man approach my car. It was like he was waiting for me to get out. I stepped out onto the sidewalk, and he asked me immediately if I had any money for food. I could smell the strong odor of alcohol on this man. All I had was about seven dollars and fifty cents in my pocket. I told him to follow me to get him some food. We walked to the nearest food place, but everything on the menu was more than eight dollars. We began walking to find something else. Young college students were bar-hopping and going from club to club all around us.

Suddenly, I felt the compassion of the Lord fill my heart for this man, and I stopped walking, looked him in the eye, and said to him, "Jesus loves you and sees you."

He responded with what I'm sure was his usual response when someone mentions God: "Yeah. I know about God."

I repeated myself three times saying, "No, you don't understand. Jesus loves you and sees you." We were standing in the middle of the sidewalk, people passing us on both sides. Suddenly, his eyes changed, and for the first time he really looked at me. I looked into his eyes and could see the little boy that the Father loved. His eyes glossed over, and tears began to fall. He collapsed on my chest and began to weep bitterly, very loudly, with snot pouring out onto my shirt. I did what you're supposed to do. I held him and wrapped my arms around him and let him weep. People were staring at us, but we didn't care. I blessed him and prayed over him. He left fully encouraged and filled with peace. We were so moved by God that we completely forgot about the food!

Sometimes we can forget that despite how we feel God is loving people all around us. In fact, there are always people around us who are hurting and dying. The Lord wants to love them through us. It's what it means to follow Jesus. He always stopped for the one who needed Him and loved them which changed their lives forever. I'm sure you can remember the time God loved you the same way through someone. If you haven't, you get the privilege to *become* that someone to another.

PRAYER

"Jesus, help us to love those around us just like we love you. We want to be your hands and feet Lord. We want to display your kindness and goodness to the lost and broken no matter if they are rich or poor. Soften our hearts God and give us compassion like we have never known. Father take us deep into your affections and show us your ways. In Jesus's name. Amen."

CHAPTER 10

LOVING GOD

God doesn't want you to love Him for what He can do for you or just for how He makes you feel. He wants you to love Him for who He is. How He makes you feel is a blessing from just knowing Him.

My heart and motives were exposed when I was in jail. I remember laying in an eight by ten concrete box with nine men stuffed inside, lying on the floor with a metal toilet beside us. Their voices echoing off the walls all at the same time. It was difficult to even hear my own thoughts. One thing was immediately evident—secret place time with the Lord was not a possibility, and that reality almost made my spirit leave me.

I pulled my sheet over my head and whispered to the Lord, "Get me out of here! I can't be here." Then the Lord spoke to me by showing me all of the promises that He has ever spoken to me, and then He asked me, "If you never left this place, spent the rest of your life here in this little room and never saw any promise I've spoken to you come to pass, would I be enough for you? Would I satisfy you?"

That reality went straight through me and exposed me from the inside out. All of my flesh screamed, "*No!*" But out of my spirit from the deepest part of my being, I spoke, "Yes."

He spoke again to me and said, "Okay. We have work to do."

I turned to the man next to me and began sharing Jesus with him. He was called away by the guard, so I looked to the young man next to him and said, "Did you hear what I told him?"

He nodded his head yes.

I said, "Do you want that? Do you want Jesus?"

He said that his nickname back home was Satan because he was evil to everyone. I began to pray for him as he repented for his sins and received Jesus as his Lord and savior. Demons came screaming out of him, and he shook violently. After he was delivered, his countenance changed, and all the pain in his body was gone. He was in jail for pulling a shotgun on an arresting police officer and with his record would be spending many years in jail. I prophesied to him and told him that Jesus was going to set him free and gave him specific instructions on what God wanted him to do when he was released. Just days later, he was released and born again into a new life in Christ.

Then the Lord spoke to me and said, "Eman, I want you to pray for everyone in here." I started with the loudest, roughest inmate, and as I prayed for him, he began to weep. He was a cold-blooded murderer and was only seventeen years old. I ended up baptizing him with three cups of water. I prayed for everyone in the jail as the Lord commanded me. I held Bible studies every day and discipled one inmate to replace me in leading the Bible studies after I left.

The day before I was released, I asked the Lord why He sent me to jail. The Lord reminded me of a prayer I prayed just a few days before I was wrongfully arrested. I told Jesus I wanted to know Him more, not for what He could do for me or promises to be fulfilled but to know Him for who He is. Right after reminding me of this, the Lord said to me, "Eman, I visit those in jail." A love for these men filled me that was not there before. Initially, I was just being obedient, but now I could see that each one of these inmates was the "least of these" and being the least, they were Christ. He was letting the scripture come alive in my heart in real time.

"As you have done to the least of these you have done it unto Me" *(Matthew 25:40).*

Jesus wants us to love Him for who He is not for what He can do for us. He visits those in jail. When you see an inmate on the side of the road, cleaning up trash for the state, do you think to yourself, *I'm so glad that's not me. Poor guy…he must have messed up his life. I wonder what he did?* Or do you ignore what your eyes are seeing altogether like that person doesn't even exist? The least of these and how you treat them is how you're treating Jesus. We must not think of ourselves as better than anyone else because that mindset will blind us to the heart of God toward others.

Jesus revealed to me my motives while in jail. I was seeking God for what He could do for me for promises to be fulfilled. While I was asking God my questions, He was asking me a question. "Eman, am I enough for you? Do I, Jesus, satisfy you completely? Would you even deny yourself my promises and truly put it on the altar not knowing if I would give you a ram in the bush? Could you settle it in your heart that the promise is going to die and believe that I am more than enough for you?" Sometimes only a "testing of your faith" will reveal to you who you're really made of and where your heart really lies. I believe that the testing of our faith is more precious than fine gold or silver and reveals to us that we truly trust and love God more than anything else, even His promises. The problem is that everyone already knows the end of the story about Abraham. Everyone knows God didn't let him kill his promised child. Although Abraham didn't know, he was fully prepared, in his heart, to kill his promise on the altar and believed that God would raise him from the dead. However, most people never settle it in their hearts to lose that promise and put it on the altar. They already expect to get it back and, in turn, never really put it on the altar of God. We must be a people who love God so much that we are willing to give up everything for Him—jobs, money, family, children belongings, and even promises and ministries. We must do this, settling in our hearts that just *knowing* Jesus is more than enough. He is completely satisfying and fulfilling.

Emotions should not dictate our relationship with the Lord. I love feeling the Lord's love and presence, but my emotions are not my anchor in our relationship. His love for me is expressed on the cross, and my love for Him is expressed in my obedience. These are my anchors.

Knowing your significant other is the greatest expression and essence of any relationship. I'm speaking about the "knowing" in your deep inner self who the person in front of you truly is. With

God, you may say, "I know I really need you, God, to do this or that." Say that God does everything you want Him to do. Say that He fulfills every personal promise to you. Does that make you know Him more? Your relationship with God cannot be based on what He does for you or what you do for Him. What can you give God if you have already given Him your life? The issue is not *doing* more to fix the disconnect you might feel in your heart toward Him. The problem is that you're not in love with Him. If you were in love with Him, nothing would be able to stop you from running into His arms and talking to Him every day, walking with Him. Obedience is just a reflection of the love that burns in you for Him, without a second thought. But obedience is not the foundation of our love. It's the action. Knowing Him is the foundation, which takes spending time with Him, just like in your marriage or any relationship you're in. Unconditional love doesn't seek its own desire. It is patient and kind.

We want to know Jesus. Paul put it like this in Philippians 3:7–11,

> *Indeed, I count everything as loss because of the surpassing worth of knowing Christ Jesus, my Lord. For His sake I have suffered the loss of all things and count them as rubbish, in order that I may gain Christ and be found in Him, not having a righteousness of my own that comes from the law, but that which comes through faith in Christ, the righteousness from God that depends on faith that I may know him and the power of His resurrection, and may share His sufferings, becoming like Him in His death, that by any means possible I may attain the resurrection from the dead.*

Jesus places the importance of knowing Him at the highest value. Matthew 7:21 says,

> *Not everyone who says to me, "Lord, Lord," will enter the kingdom of heaven. But the one who*

does the will of my Father who is in heaven. On that day many will say to me, "Lord, Lord, did we not prophesy in your name, and cast out demons in your name, and do many mighty works in your name!" And then will I declare to them. 'I never knew you; depart from me, you workers of lawlessness.

Jesus actually defines lawlessness as not knowing Him or obeying the will of the Father. If we really knew Jesus, we would put the deeds of the flesh to death.

The walk of knowing and falling in love with Jesus is the one that my heart most desires, to love Him with everything that I am. What a reality! My question is, "God, how can I love you with everything that I am?" His answer is, "By first believing who I say you are." The divine nature of God is *love*. We have been reconciled back to the Father through the blood of Jesus. We were created to look just like Him.

I remember one day that I was in a group meeting and the Lord showed me something that has changed my entire perspective on my identity as a child in His kingdom. He showed me a picture of a baby being born. Then He said, "Eman, this baby is born in the country it's born into. As it grows, it does not question its citizenship. Why?"

I said, "Tell me."

He replied, "Because the child was born in that country. As the child grows, does it have a list of things it must do to maintain citizenship? No, because citizenship is not based on what you do or don't do. Your citizenship is solely based on the fact that you were born in the country you were born into. Your citizenship is your birthright. It's the same in my kingdom. Because you were born into it, there is no list of demands or things you must do every day to maintain your citizenship in my kingdom. Eman, how long is a pregnancy?"

I answered, "Nine months."

He asked me, "So how long is that compared to a lifetime?"

I said, "Well, not very long. It's very short."

He responded, "That's right. You are in the womb of eternity, learning how to become love. You are in the womb of eternity, being formed to look just like me, just as if you were being formed in your mother's womb, being formed to resemble your parents. You are being formed in this life to look just like me, to look just like love."

PRAYER

Father, give us the faith to believe we are your children accepted into your kingdom and being formed to look just like love. Give us vision to understand with our hearts and minds that there is nothing we must do to earn this but that it is who you have made us this way. Help us, Holy Spirit, to rest in the reality that we are yours. In Jesus's name. Amen.

CHAPTER 11

THE JOY OF THE LORD

Joy is when your faith meets the truth. When you believe the true reality, loving righteousness and hating evil, then joy manifests. It is the rightful position of every king in His kingdom. It is the attitude of a true believer, the weapon of choice. We must abide in the joy of the Lord. We must remain in a constant state of gladness of heart no matter what. The importance of being glad of heart is clearly stated in James.

> *Count it all joy, my brothers when you meet trials of various kinds, for you know that the testing of your faith produces steadfastness. And let steadfastness have its full effect, that you may be perfect and complete, lacking in nothing. (James 1:2–4)*

If the joy of the Lord is our strength, then it must be what Jesus walked in, even as He faced trials that we, also, are promised to go through. The testing of our faith propels us into steadfastness, making us immovable. The word *steadfastness* here, means firm, persistent, and committed to one's endeavors. It will make us firm in our faith and determined not to submit to the lies of the enemy but believe the truth we have in Jesus. According to God's Word, joy is the reaction that He wants in us when we meet trials of various kinds. So let us remain in His joy. Let us ask and call upon the Holy Spirit, who reveals all truths to us, to teach us and train us in the joy of the Lord. I'm reminded of Jesus after His first sermon when they tried to stone Him and throw Him off a cliffside. Yet we know that Jesus was known as a man of great joy.

"You have loved righteousness and hated wickedness; therefore God, your God, has anointed you with the oil of Joy beyond your companions" *(Hebrews 1:9).*

The Word says it was the joy set before Him that He endured the cross (see Hebrews 12:2). Suffering is a fruit of God's Spirit. We cannot separate the joy of the Lord on earth without enduring suffering and hardships. We all have different levels of suffering depending on where we live. For example, suffering for someone in America may differ drastically from the suffering of someone in a third-world country who grew up surrounded by war on their own land. Suffering is relative to the person it comes to. Likewise, what a hardship is for *me* may be different from a hardship for a billionaire. It is all relative.

Suffering and joy are divinely married to one another. I believe suffering that does not produce patience and the joy of the Lord is just suffering in vain. The Spirit of God has been poured out into our hearts and comes with all His fruits and attributes. The soil of our hearts must be broken up, and seeds implanted in it must die in order for the tree to grow. Patience becomes perfected as the branches must grow strong enough in the waiting in order to hold the fruit that grows on it.

The Lord exemplified this more than anyone, receiving the greatest fruit of suffering than anyone by redeeming the world back to the Father through the cross. That same principle applies to us but in a lesser degree. We actually are called to be glorified with Jesus as we suffer with Him.

> *[A]nd if children, then heirs—heirs of God and fellow heirs with Christ, provided we suffer with him in order that we may also be glorified with him. For I consider that the sufferings of this present time are not worth comparing with the glory that is to be revealed to us. (Romans 8:17)*

Truly, the joy of the Lord is our strength. The key for this joy from heaven to manifest in us is by embracing our cross, enduring suffering, and being glorified with Christ as children of God.

I pray that every hardship and suffering that you endure may produce the fruit of joy with patience and power. I bless you that the things that you have endured for Christ may manifest Christ more completely in you and bring you higher to a place of great joy and hope in Jesus's name.

CHAPTER 12

WALKING IN LOVE

Love has many different facets and attributes, but there is a foundation that love thrives from. This foundation enables us, as followers of Christ, to shine brightly and be good ambassadors of the love of Jesus. I'm not saying that this is exactly how love works because we know that God is deeper and vaster than eternity itself. He cannot be quantified or defined in any human language. He does, however, give us pretext and guidelines that set us up and establish us in the way of truth which empowers us to walk like Jesus.

The most fascinating attribute of God, which I believe is a central pillar for walking in love, is that He has the power and authority to *not only* forgive us but to remember our transgressions no more! This is an incredible truth that we need to abide in daily. He forgives and forgets! Our Heavenly Father desires and chooses to look at us with an unblemished perspective by the blood of Jesus. What would it look like if we truly kept no record of wrongs against anyone, including ourselves? What if we, like God, look at others through the blood of Jesus?

If we hold no record of wrongs against ourselves or anyone else, then we begin walking in true love. There wouldn't be a need for anyone to ask you for forgiveness. You would not hold people to a standard that they must meet in order for you to love them. This would cause us to actively walk in and release the reality of grace everywhere we go with whoever we meet, including ourselves. Paul wrote,

> *But with me it is a very small thing that I should be judged by you or by any human court. In fact, I do not even judge myself. Nor am I aware of anything against myself,* (1 Corinthians 4:3–4)

God has made a way for us to walk in His grace toward others. There is a way that "seems right to man." There is a common phrase that we grew up hearing and have likely said ourselves. "I'll forgive, but I'll never forget." This is false wisdom and is contradictory to the teachings of Jesus and the instruction of God. The Word is clear that we are to keep no record of wrongs against one another as this is a part of walking in love. How can we remember transgressions against us by others but say we forgave them? This is not true forgiveness. True forgiveness forgets the wrongdoing completely. Now, we may remember in our *minds* but our hearts do not (see Chapter 13, "The New Heart and New Spirit"). Of course, this is impossible by human effort. We need the power of the Holy Spirit to walk in this truth and reality of God's heart in our lives. We can do nothing apart from God. We need the Holy Ghost alive and active in us. We need to be aware of His power and presence every day. You can look back over your life and even the history of your city, town, or country and see how things would look totally different if people walked in the power of the Holy Spirit to keep no record of wrongs against anyone. The courts would be empty! It's revolutionary, it's God's will and desire, and most exciting of all, it's possible and available for us all! Think of anyone you know that you are holding a record of wrongs against, even if that person is yourself or God. Take a moment for this.

If you want to truly walk in the power and love of the Holy Spirit, ask Jesus to baptize you in the love, power, joy, and fire of the Holy Spirit. Ask Jesus to give you a new heart, His heart flowing with rivers of living water. Ask Him to renew your mind and give you a brand new consciousness, made clean and washed by his blood. God is faithful, and he will give you what you have asked for. Have faith and don't doubt. If you ask Him, you will receive the Holy Spirit. He will give you this gift! Ask already believing you'll receive it, and you will!

LETTING HIM IN

What good is prayer without faith? What good is faith without love? People clamor at the slightest hint of chaos, yet the very thing they grasp for has come into the world and is right at hand. He is at our door; love is knocking. Will we not open that door? Will we mute our ears to the pounding sound of His pursuit of our home, which He purchased with His own blood? Who makes a purchase at their own expense but does not gratify Himself to what is rightfully His? Instead, he knocks with invitation in hand. In patience, love has come to us with a relationship that redefines intimacy as we know it. Will we stare through our peepholes and pretend that we don't hear that knock that shakes through every heart? Or will we *believe* and let the homeowner into *all* of His new house? Don't grasp to take hold of disillusioned thoughts of peace. The peace of this world is not actually peace at all. Peace, hope, and joy are one—Jesus Christ.

God's love toward us is unconditional. Our love toward Him should be the same. I believe that a lot of the church's love toward the Father is conditional based on whether He is blessing them, making things comfortable, or prospering them on this earth. Read Haggai 1.

Selflessness is required in order for love to thrive in the kingdom of God. To truly love people with supernatural love, selflessness must be established. The only reason you would become selfless is because you have believed that the life of Jesus is far greater than your own, which it is. He gave His life up to give it to you! Jesus gave His life for us so that we could live out His life in place of our own. We get to become living sacrifices.

So many times we look at the apostle Paul's definition of "love" as a list of things to compare ourselves to. We envision as a list of godly attributes that we will always fall short of but use as the outline for wishful thinking.

Love is patient and kind; love does not envy
or boast; it is not arrogant or rude. It does not insist
on its own way; it is not irritable or resentful; it
does not rejoice at wrongdoing, but rejoices with the
truth. Love bears all things, believes all things, hopes
all things, and endures all things. Love never fails.

I will tell you the truth. This is not a list of wishful thinking. This is an identity list. We were made in the very same likeness and image of God. We were created to look just like our dad. He is love, and so are we. This is who we are, not what we are to aspire to. It is integrated into our new Heavenly DNA because we believe in Jesus. When you believed in Jesus, your DNA changed to that of heaven. Your blood type changed to JC positive, and your family tree became the cross on Calvary. Your heritage is the throne room of grace. Every cell in your body is energized with the glory of God and wants to manifest that glory and shine like the sun! Jesus said, "Let it be on earth as it is in heaven." This is not something to come in *after* we die, this is a "here and now" statement. He was saying, "As it is in heaven, so it will be on earth." In fact, the whole earth groans and suffers pains for the time when the children of God shall be manifested in the glory prepared for them. Through love by the power of the Holy Spirit, this is all possible.

The Lord wants us to consider ourselves as who He says we are. I believe one of the biggest lies of the enemy is trying to blind people from the reality of their true identities as sons and daughters of the king. His worst fear is that we will believe who God says we are and look just like Jesus. The enemy is afraid that we will believe we are righteous. We are kings, sitting at the right hand of the Father with the Lord, having every spiritual blessing, and filled fully with the fullness of Christ. He is terrified that we will step into joy unspeakable and start recognizing his tactics and schemes, which have been the same from the beginning. He is a liar. His fiery darts are lies. He shoots them right at us and camouflages them to look like other people coming against us. This way, we can't see that he is the one attacking us. He attacks our minds, and his motive is destruction by stealing what Jesus has given back to us—our identity. He whispers lies like, "I'm just so stressed out right now. I'm always going to be alone. No one will ever love me. I'm not beautiful. They think this about me and that about me. He or she doesn't really love me." He is the king of sowing suspicion and doubt to keep us from seeing people by the spirit, through the blood and redemption in Christ. He attempts to get us to see people in the flesh, which is against God. He will try to get us to question all our relationships by planting seeds of doubt. He wants us so focused in ourselves, so focused inwardly that we don't see who is right in front of us. Jesus is right there with all the love of the Father to cover us and consume us and the people He has placed in our lives to love and for us to love them is right in front of us as well.

You can't try to be something you already are. Contend in the secret place to know His love more. In the face of lies, proclaim the truth. This is standing in faith. Consider yourself holy. Consider yourself righteous. Consider yourself not a sinner. Consider yourself dead to sin. Consider yourself a son or daughter in the kingdom. Consider yourself a friend of God. Consider yourself filled with the fullness of Christ and given every spiritual blessing. Consider yourself above and not beneath. Consider yourself covered in His grace and goodness. Consider yourself loved and consider yourself free. Because you are all these things and more! When you wake up tomorrow, these are the things that are true. He truly does live in us if we believe in the name of Jesus. We become one with the Father and the Spirit dwells in us. Love is not conditional. If it is, it is not love at all. We can be perfected to love unconditionally, although it is a process. God's motive is always love and, therefore, should also be ours!.

PRAYER

Lord, help us believe in the identity that you paid for us. Jesus, renew our minds in your truth and transform us by that truth in the power of your Spirit. Amen.

CHAPTER 13

THE NEW HEART
AND NEW SPIRIT

What is it that God wants from us? It's the thing He searches out in every man. He knows it well. It's His motive in every action toward us. Our heart is what He is after. When He gets your heart, He gets all of you. The heart is the place God extends His invitation for romance and intimacy toward us. He actually desires to create in us a clean heart that is perfectly designed by Him to receive the love He has for us—a place where he can live and set up His throne so he can commune with us. This new heart is completely undeserved. There is absolutely nothing you can do for God to earn this amazing gift.

Time and time again, people search for fulfillment in this world. People spend their whole lives trying to earn, achieve, and be successful according to the standards of this world. They allow the words of man to become greater than the Word of God. His Word is greater than any words a human could ever speak. It's eternal and will never end. People seek in so many places other than the one place that could ever bring them any real change that extends into eternity. Jesus is the Word made flesh. He came to give us life to the fullest. To know Jesus is to know God the Father. He wants us to know Him and to respond to His love made clear by the cross of Calvary.

> *And I will give them one heart [a new heart]
> and I will put a new spirit within them; and I will
> take the stony [unnaturally hardened] heart out
> of their flesh, and will give them a heart of flesh
> [sensitive and responsive to the touch of their god].
> (Ezekiel 11:19 AMP)*

There is a promise from God that He will actually come inside of a person and recreate a new heart in them. Jesus spoke of this new heart and applied the faith factor.

"Whoever believes in me, as the scripture has said, 'Out of his heart will flow rivers of living water'" (John 7:38).

It's by faith in Jesus that guarantees us living water. The same place where the rivers of living water flow from is the same place we receive our new heart from the Lord. In this place of eternal abiding, His peace is present. This peace surpasses all understanding. The key to peace is given to us in Philippians 4:7.

> *Be anxious for nothing, but in everything, by
> prayer and petition, with thanksgiving, present your
> requests to God. and the peace of God, which sur-
> passes all understanding, will guard your hearts and
> your minds in Christ Jesus.*

This new heart comes just as we talked about in chapter 5 about resting in this love.

His love is like a vast ocean. It is so deep that nobody can know the depths or swim to the bottom of it without losing their own life. That's the cost of his love. You cannot swim to the bottom of the ocean in your own power. At some point, you must be crushed by the weight of His glory in the depths of His love. Then you will be carried away to the bottom by the power that surrounds you. One must lose his life to find it, and then you will begin to truly know the depths of His love. You can't get there on your own. What are your muscles, your bones, your mind, or your strength? The Helper is here, let Him help. He is mighty. Stop struggling and resisting Him.

Let yourself sink into His depths. Lose your life in Him. Let him love you. You're worth loving.

The new heart and spirit is a supernatural event. Now that Jesus has been glorified, this isn't just a nice thought or suggestion from God. He doesn't just say things and not follow through with what He says He will do. He is not a man that He should lie. No, He cannot lie (see Numbers 23:19)!

On April 13 and 14 of 2013, I was at a church meeting where a young man was preaching for the weekend. I had never heard of Him and actually argued with God on attending this meeting. Some would ask how I could argue with God, especially if I knew it was God speaking. I would ask that person if they have ever known someone loved them, but they didn't love them back the same way. When that person speaks to you, it's just annoying because you know their motives. They love you and want a relationship with you, but you don't love them. So every word out of their mouth just rubs you the wrong way. It's aggravating. Well, that's what my relationship with God was like at that time. He loved me with everything, but I didn't love Him like that. He kept on telling me about the meeting. I was just getting very annoyed, so finally I obliged so He would leave me alone. So I went to the meeting. You see, God doesn't need you in the best condition to set you up for a gift that He wants to give you. If He wants to do something in you, it will happen no matter your attitude. He is not intimidated.

At that time, I was what most would call a hypocrite. I was raised in the church, and I knew Jesus was real, but I was not following Him nor was I in love with Him. He was in love with me, though, and that seems to make all the difference when it comes to encountering Him as I was soon to experience.

I had the worst attitude as I sat down in my seat. I was judging the worship. I was judging the pastor. I was criticizing everything. God loves us beyond our inability to love Him or anything or anyone else. I was twisted and warped in my thinking, and I was hurt and wounded in my heart. I had just been through a season for the last three years where my wife had left me and divorced me for my older brother. I didn't really have a positive outlook on my life, although God did wonders in my heart in the arena of forgiveness toward them both when it happened. However, because of my circumstances, I was blind to the miracles that God had already been performing in my life.

When the preacher was introduced, there was an eruption of applause and a standing ovation. I was disgusted at the sound of such praise for a mere man. I thought, *He's just a man, that's not right!* Then my thoughts to myself turned to a whisper in my friends' ear next to me. "That's not right, he is just a man." Surely this guy was a prideful and glory-hungry man to receive such praise. As he approached the stage to preach, I was sure he was going to say nothing that I would like. Then he spoke, and the first words out of his mouth were "That's not right. That's not right. Jesus help," choking back tears. I was astonished! God had my complete and undivided attention after that.

As he began to preach, it almost seemed like I was hearing something I had heard my entire life although it was different. I remember wondering, *Why is this different from the gospel I grew up with?* As I tuned in, I realized what it was. The first thing that I realized was what he preached was coming from a man who was actually walking like Jesus. I didn't know him, but I knew he must be living what he was preaching. The second thing was that it really seemed like good news! I realized my whole life, it seemed I had heard the news part, but it never seemed good. This was *really* good news! So I prayed a simple prayer. "God, give me a new heart so I can love people how you love them and see people how you see them. God, give me a new mind. Sin consciousness, leave! God, I thank you for a pure conscience that is purified by your blood."

That night, I went to my mother's house where I was staying and fell asleep on the couch. At this time, I was over 480 lbs. I had sleep apnea, and I didn't sleep well. When I laid down that night to sleep, I slept through the whole night which I'd never really experienced. The rest and sleep I had was so indescribable. It was like I was sleeping in heaven itself. When I woke up from this miracle sleep, I noticed something different immediately. My first thought was, *Alien!* There was something in me that was not from me, and

I knew I had nothing to do with what was happening to me. I was completely overwhelmed by this thing in me. It was like a raging river; every cell in my body was surging with power. It was so intense that I lost my breath. My next breath was like the first breath I had ever taken in my life. I was pulsating with this energy and power that I had never known or even knew existed. I am now familiar with this phenomenon, but at that moment, it was like crashing waves washing over and vibrating through every nerve and molecule in my body—beginning in my heart and pulsating outward in every direction. It was the frequency of heaven, the heartbeat of the throne room of grace. Activated by the manifestation of the presence of the king, it was cleansing me and invigorating my soul and spirit as this overwhelming love was being poured out in me. That very moment, I lost my breath. Right then I realized that I was truly alive now! Before that moment, I was dead and didn't know it. I was an unbelieving believer and hypocrite before that moment.

I looked around to see if anyone was around and experiencing what I was experiencing, but I was alone on the couch. As I looked out the window, God opened my eyes, and I went into an open vision. I didn't even know what that was at the time. It was all new to me. I saw people from every nation and tongue—men, women, children, young and old. This raging river inside of me was pouring out to them all. The love of the Father was rushing out of me and washing over everyone!

I was in shock, and then the fear of God came down on me. I said, "Lord, it's all true! The Bible is true! Lord, please don't take this love away from me. I didn't know this was real, but now I know! Please let this always be with me. It's too good to live without!" I didn't understand then what I was asking for, but I've since learned more about what I was asking of God. His love is unfailing and unending. It's always faithful to us in every situation and in every circumstance. If we can trust in Him and lean on Him with our entire character and personality, fully relying on Him to be there for us because He is alive and He loves us, then we will experience true life in Christ and life to the fullest!

The first thing I wanted to do with my new heart and river of love was wash my mom's dishes. Now, this was truly a revival! This was a war my whole life. I hated doing dishes. But I walked into the kitchen and joyfully began to wash the dishes. Suddenly I felt like a drunk man and almost fell over backwards. It was the first time I had experienced being drunk in the spirit, and it was during an act of service, which has now become my life—to serve, go low, and love everyone everywhere I am while loving Jesus.

I decided after my encounter and washing my mom's dishes that I wanted to see miracles like Jesus did in the Bible. So I went for a walk. It was springtime, so lots of people were outside, and I went to anyone I could. People were healed on the first day, which began a journey in power evangelism that has never ended and will continue until I am with the Lord in glory. If you see a brother in need and you *have* to give but you don't give but rather close your heart off to him, how is the love of the Father within you?

If you would like this new heart and new spirit, ask Jesus right now in your own words. Ask Him for a new heart filled with His love and ask Him to renew your mind and give you a clear, white-as-snow consciousness. His love will remove your old heart, which is filled with memories of past life wounds, and He will put in you a new heart. With that new heart will come new memories of the things in heaven—things that are lovely and good memories in your heart with Christ. You will still remember past hurts but only in your mind so you can share the testimony of what God has done for you. Your new heart will not feel those pains from the past any longer. May you be free from this world by your new heart in Christ and new spirit by *His* Spirit. Be filled and be free in Jesus's name.

> *There is a love, a love that flows from the breathe of a King,*
> *There is a love, a love that is unmatched by any storm.*
> *There is a love that is unmatched by any flame or quake of the earth.*

This love flows from the breath of the Son of the Living God.

The breath of life flows into the hearts of man, blowing away all darkness to reveal a light.

A light that pierces through the shadows in this world.

There is a love, a love soaked in the power and person of God, crushing the works of the enemy.

Giving victory to us who believe in the name of Jesus, for He is our hope, our Saviour and our beautiful friend.

ABOUT THE AUTHOR

Eman Norman is from Lexington, Kentucky. He is the youngest son of four and grew up in Lexington most of his life. At the age of twenty-eight, he had a dramatic encounter with God that caused him to become a minister, missionary, and evangelist, traveling all over the United States with the mission to bring the Gospel to as many people as he could and encouraging local churches to step out to reach the lost with the gospel of Jesus Christ.

CPSIA information can be obtained
at www.ICGtesting.com
Printed in the USA
LVHW030100080821
694192LV00001B/40

9 781098 066895